Mikiko Nakamoto

School Life

Let's communicate in English!

APRICOT

ラーニングワールドシリーズは全9巻からなり、幼児から中学生まで、それぞれの発達段階と学習年数に応じてフレキシブルに使っていただけるように構成されています。
本シリーズはヒューマニスティックアプローチとコミュニカティブ・アプローチを取り入れ、従来の暗記とパターンプラクティス中心の英語教育ではなく、「答えが1つでない」英語による言語教育を目指しています。子供達の発話に重要な「自分の意見の構築」「自尊心の育成」「他者への許容」等が英語の四技能の学習を通して習得できます。
本書 READY for Learning Worldはカナダ、タイ、メキシコ、中国の9-10歳の子供達を設定し、各ユニットはその子供達の学校生活の場面で構成されています。各場面に適した語彙やダイアログに加え、チャンツやボキャブラリーソングで楽しく効果的に英語が身に付くようデザインしました。各ユニットの6ページ目には国際理解、自己表現、プレゼンテーション能力を育成するための活動が付いています。
本書はLearning World 1または2終了時に効果的に使用することができます。2021年度の改訂版ではアルファベットの母音、子音の音を強化し、Achievement Targetsを一部改訂しました。

このテキストには、つぎのマークが入っています。なにをするのか、みてわかるようになりましょう。

Scene of the Unit
日常よくある場面です。どんな話をしているのでしょう。

Words
場面ごとに出てくる重要語彙です。

Dialogue
すぐに使える会話です。
よくきいて覚えましょう。

Chant
リズムにのっておぼえましょう。

Global Education
4つの国の友達の生活をみてみましょう。

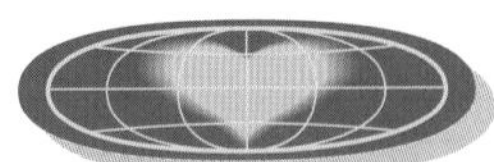

Self-Expression
自分自身のことを英語で表現しましょう。

Vocabulary song
語彙の習得のための歌です。丸ごとおぼえましょう。

Sounds of the Alphabet
アルファベットの音とつづりの関係を調べましょう。

Listening Test
英語をきいて答えましょう。
どれだけききとれるかな？

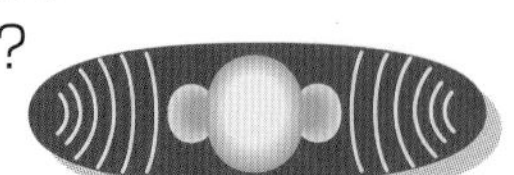

おうちで音声をききましょう。

  **3**

これだけできるようにがんばろう。

1 自分の名前、とし、住んでいるところが大きな声ではっきり言えます。
Able to say my name, my age and where I live in a loud voice.

2 likeを使って自分の好きなものがはっきり大きな声で言えます。
Able to say what I like in a loud voice.

3 自分の友達を3人紹介できます。 Able to introduce three of my friends.
This is my friend. Her(His) name is....

4 好きな学校の科目を英語で言うことができます。
Able to say what school subject I like.

5 好きな動物を英語で言うことができます。
Able to say what animal I like.

6 テキストの57ページの絵を使って自分の家族を紹介できます。
Able to introduce my family members using the picture I drew on page 57.
This is my family. I have....

7 今日の曜日と天気を英語で言うことができます。
Able to say the days of the week and today's weather.

8 会話カードのうち6枚の会話が言えます。
Able to say six dialogues from the Dialogue Cards with my friend.

9 テキストの中の vocabulary song を5つ歌えます。
Able to sing five songs from the textbook. (6) (11) (17) (23) (29) (35) (41) (47) (53) (59)

10 テキストの中の [CHANT] を6つ言えます。 (8) (14) (20) (26) (32)
Able to recite six chants from the CHANT pages. (38) (44) (50) (56) (62)

11 Wordsの欄にある絵（文字）を20大きな声で言うことができます。
Able to say 20 words from the 'Words' sections in each unit in a loud voice.

12 先生が見せる10のアルファベットを見て、そのアルファベットの音が言えます。
Able to say the sounds of ten letters my teacher shows.
(a) (b) (c) (d) (e) (f) (g) (h) (i) (j) (k) (l) (m) (n) (o) (p) (q) (r) (s) (t) (u) (v) (w) (x) (y) (z)

13 先生が見せる10枚の絵の最初の文字が言えます。
Able to say the first letters of ten pictures my teacher shows.

14 先生が見せるthree-letter-wordsを10読むことができます。
Able to say ten three-letter-words my teacher shows.

15 テキストの [CHANT] の英語をノートにすべて書きうつしました。 (8) (14) (20) (26) (32)
Copied the chants from the CHANT pages into my notebook. (38) (44) (50) (56) (62)

16 自分のことを5ついじょうの文を使ってはっきりと言うことができます。
Able to describe myself clearly using 5 or more sentences.

○の中の数字(すうじ)はページをあらわしています。

Nice to Meet You

CD 3
Hi! My name is Kaetlyn.
I am 9 years old.
I'm from Canada.
CD 4
Hi! My name is Eric.
I am 9 years old.
I'm from Mexico.

N O P Q R S T U V W X Y Z

n o p q r s t u v w x y z

CONTENTS

WELCOME
Learning World
PINK
WELCOME
Learning World
WELCOME
Learning World
Learning World 1
READY
Learning World
Learning World 2
Learning World 3
Learning World 4
BRIDGE
Learning World 5
TOMORROW

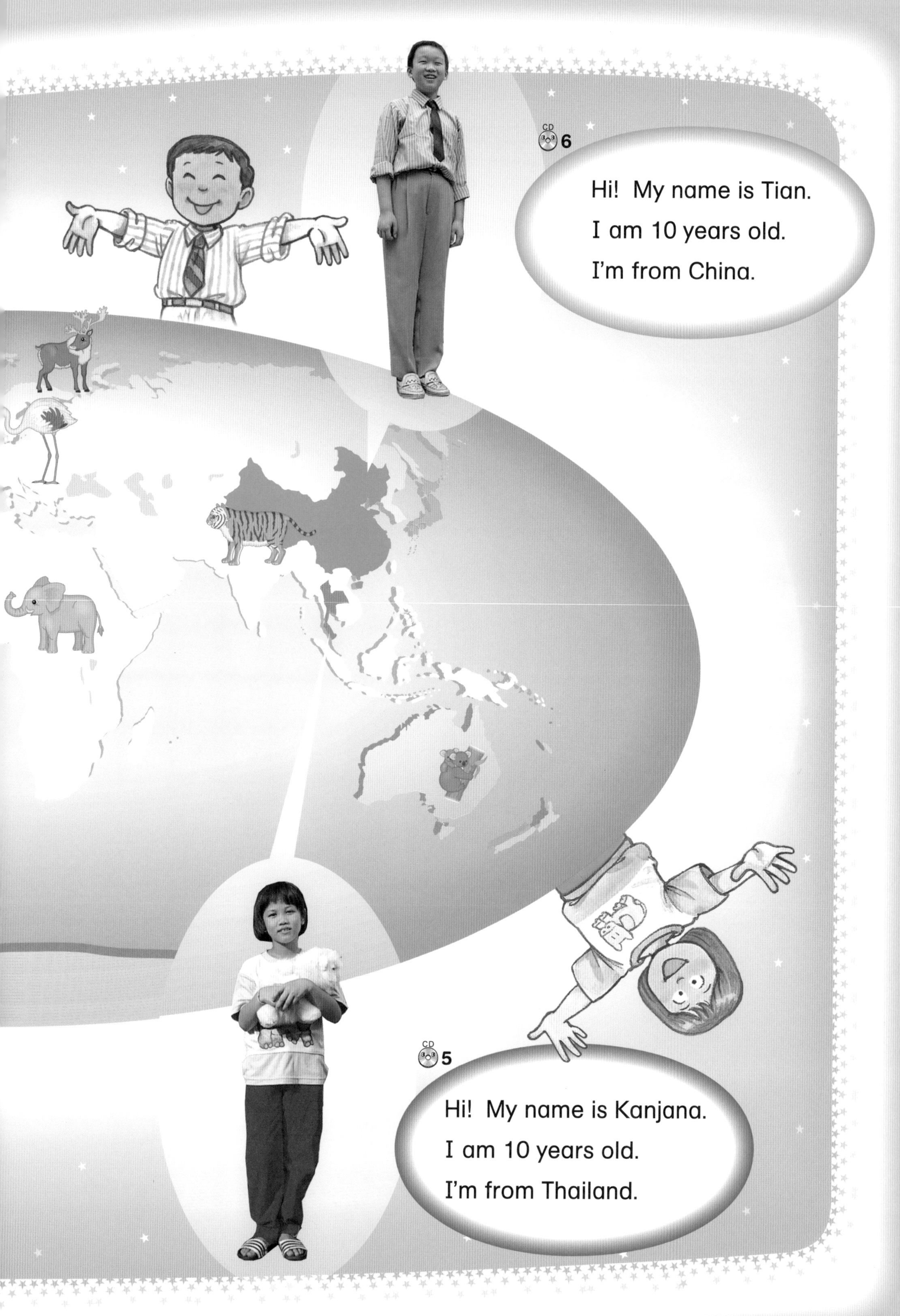
6
Hi! My name is Tian.
I am 10 years old.
I'm from China.
5
Hi! My name is Kanjana.
I am 10 years old.
I'm from Thailand.

CD 7→8

What's your name?

My name is Eric.

How old are you?

I'm ten years old.

Where do you live?

I live in Canada.

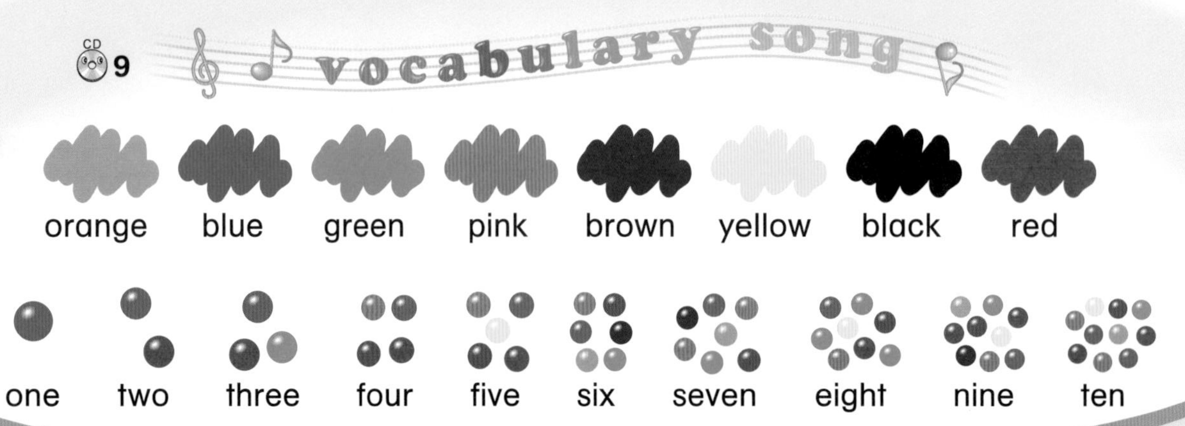

CD 10

A
yellow
B
blue
C
red
D
green
E
yellow
F
blue
G
red
H
yellow
I
blue
J
red
K
green
L
yellow
M
blue
N
red
O
yellow
P
blue
Q
red
R
green
S
yellow
T
blue
U
red
V
yellow
W
blue
X
red
Y
green
Z
blue

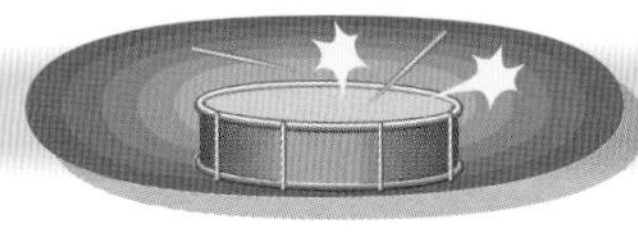

CD 11

This is Canada. Let's say Hello.

This is Mexico. Let's say Buenos dias.

This is Thailand. Let's say Sawasdee Ka.

This is China. Let's say Ni hao.

This is Japan. Let's say Konnichiwa.

Hello.

Buenos días.

สวัสดีค่ะ
Sawasdee Ka.

你好
Ni hao.

こんにちは
Konnichiwa.

Myself

This is me.

My name is ______________________.

I am ____________ years old.

I live in ______________________.

On the Way to School

SCHOOL
CD 13→14
Good morning, Mr. Takahashi.
Good morning, Kaetlyn.
How are you?
I'm fine.
CD 12
vocabulary song
Good morning.
Good afternoon.
Good evening.

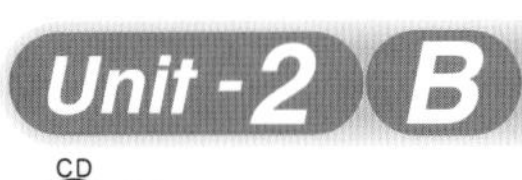

CD 15

How do you come to school?

By bus.

Good-bye.

See you later.

CD 16

Words

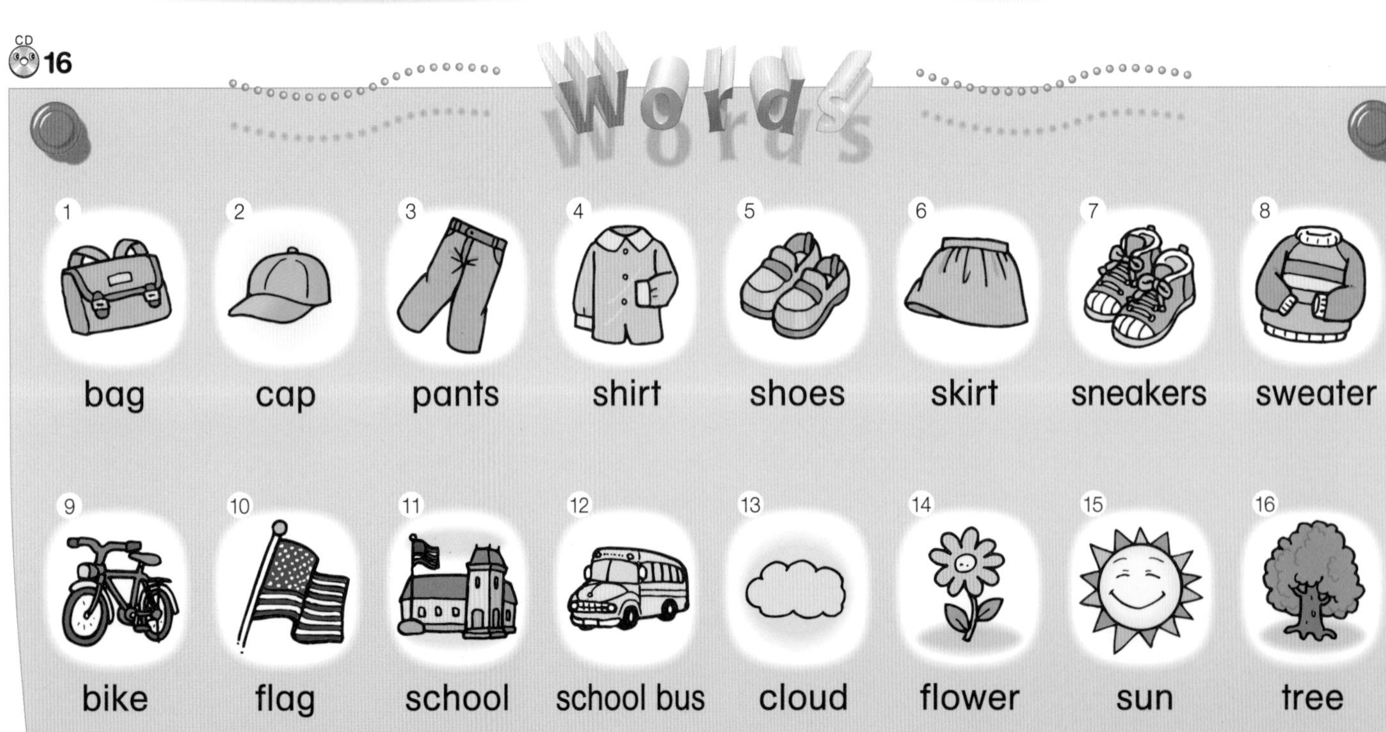

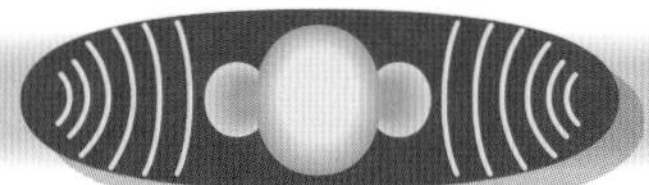

1

a

b

c

2

a

b

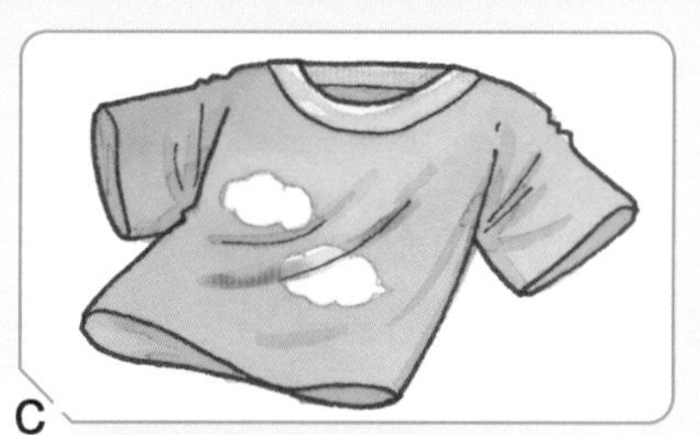
c

3

a

b

c

4

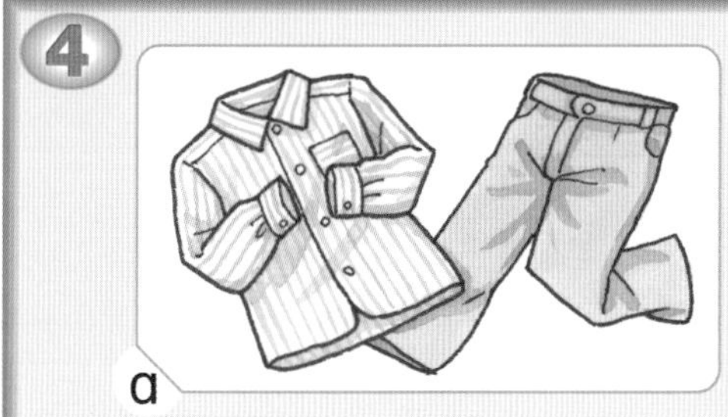
a

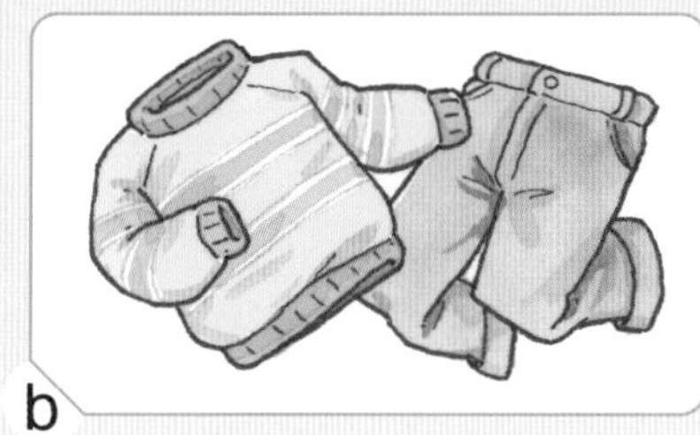
b

c

CD 17

ABCDEFGHIJKLMNOPQRSTUVWXYZ

a orange b black c green d green e orange f black g green h green

i orange j brown k blue l blue m green n blue o orange p yellow

q brown r green s green t blue u orange

v brown w yellow x green y yellow z green

a, b, c, d, e, f, g,
h, i, j, k, l, m, n,
o, p, q, r, s, t,
U are out!

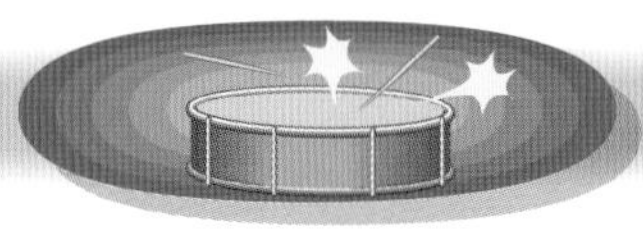

My name is Kaetlyn. What's your name?

My name is Eric. What's your name?

My name is Kanjana. What's your name?

My name is Tian. What's your name?

I'm Kaetlyn. You are Eric.

I'm Eric. You are Kanjana.

I'm Tian. You are Kaetlyn.

I'm Kanjana. You are Tian.

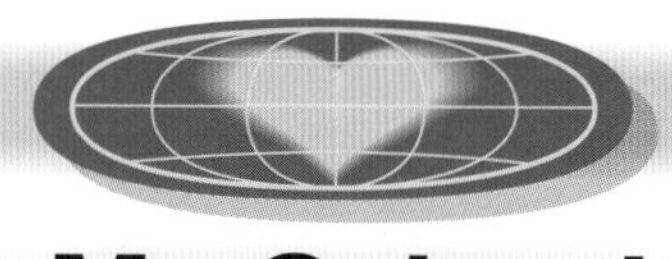

My School

CD 76

This is my school.
I go to school on foot.

This is my school.
I go to school by train.

This is my school.
I go to school by bus.

This is my school.
I go to school by bike.

This is my school.

I go to
elementary school.

I go to school .

In the Classroom

CD 19 vocabulary song

Hello.

Bonjour.

你好

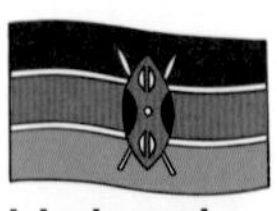
Hujambo.

Guten Tag.

CD 20→21

Good morning.
This is our new friend.
Her name is Yuko Treadway.
She is from Japan.

Hi. My name is Yuko.
Nice to meet you.

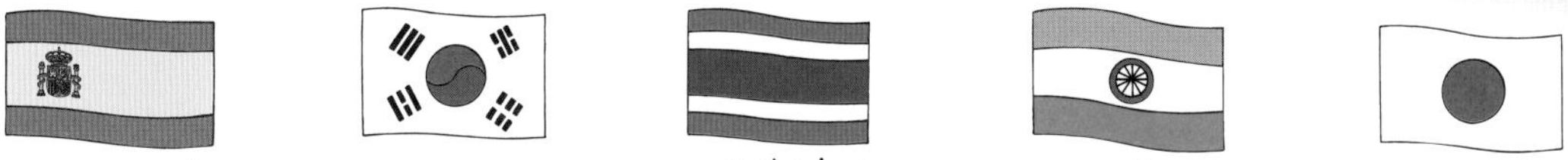

JAPAN?

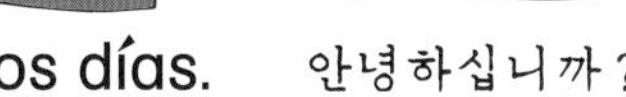

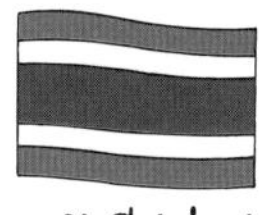

สวัสดี (ค่ะ)

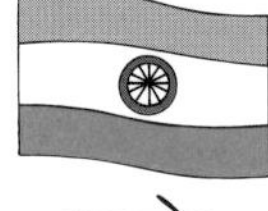

नमस्ते

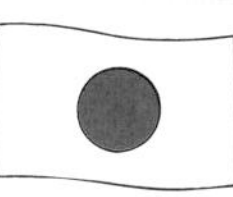

こんにちは

CD 22

What time is it?

It's nine o'clock.

Be quiet, please.

Oh, sorry.

CD 23

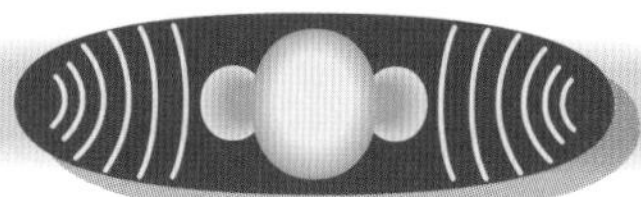

a b c

3

a b c

a b c

Let's hunt!

Let's start from a.

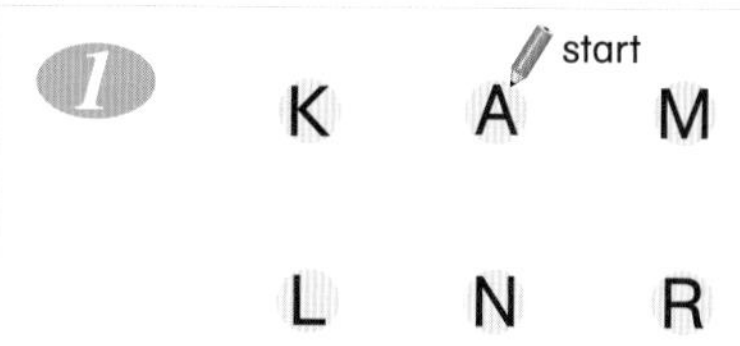

1

K	A (start)	M
L	N	R
P	O	Q

( )

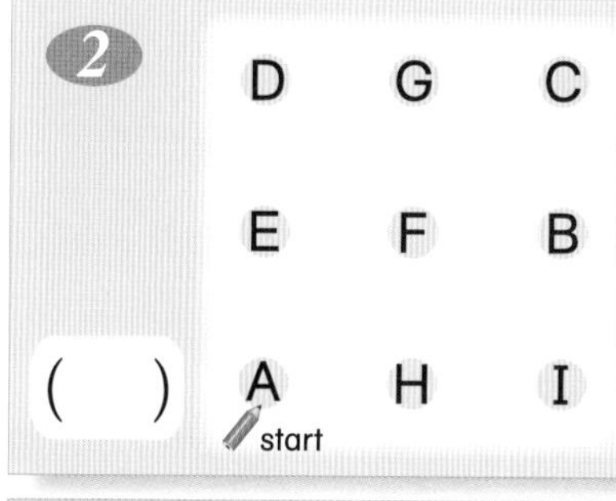

2

D	G	C
E	F	B
A (start)	H	I

( )

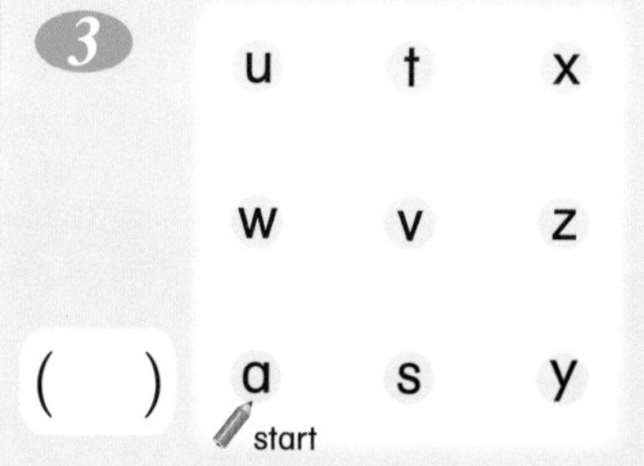

3

u	t	x
w	v	z
a (start)	s	y

( )

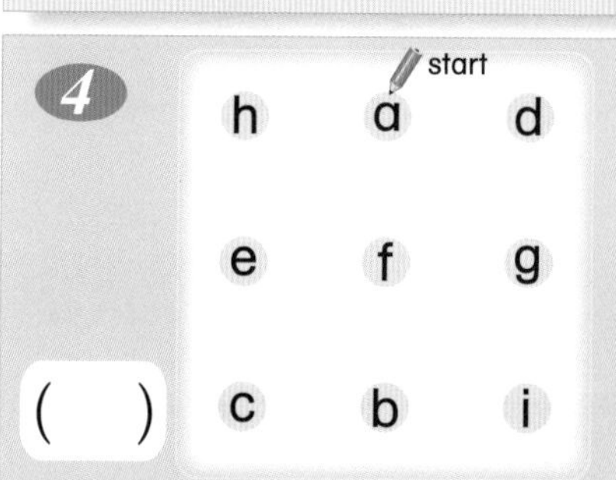

4

h	a (start)	d
e	f	g
c	b	i

( )

a 

b 

c 

d

CD 24

Tick, tock, tick, tock, what time is it?
School time, study time. It's nine o'clock.

Tick, tock, tick, tock, what time is it?
School time, study time. It's nine o'clock.

This is My Friend

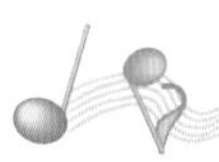

Kaetlyn

This is my friend. Her name is Kaetlyn.
Kaetlyn, Kaetlyn, Kaetlyn. My friend's name is Kaetlyn.

This is my friend. His name is Eric.
Eric, Eric, Eric. My friend's name is Eric.

Eric

My Friends

This is my friend.
Her name is Shannon.

This is my friend.
His name is Mauricio.

This is my friend.
Her name is Watcharaporn.

They are my friends.
Their names are Zhu Wei and Tang Kai.

This is my friend.

______ name is ______

At School -English Lesson-

CD 26→27

What is this in English?

It is a stapler.

CD 25 vocabulary song

Sun	Mon	Tue	Wed	Thu	Fri	Sat
Sunday	Monday	Tuesday	Wednesday	Thursday	Friday	Saturday

CD 28

May I use your eraser?

OK. Here you are.

Take out your textbook.
Open it to page eight.

OK.

CD 29

Words

1 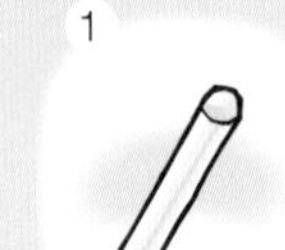 chalk	2  eraser	3  pencil	4 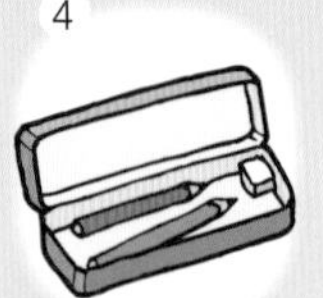 pencil case	5 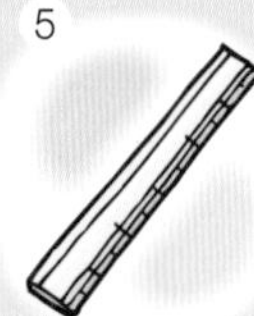 ruler	6  scissors	7  stapler	8  textbook
9  English	10  Japanese	11  math	12  music	13  P.E.	14  science	15  social studies	16  Life Environment Studies

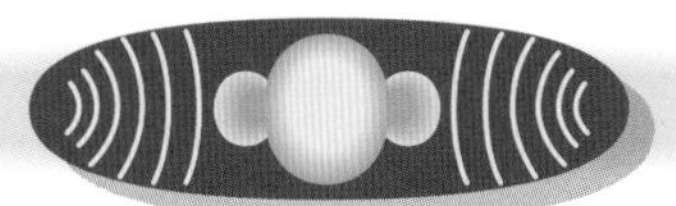

1

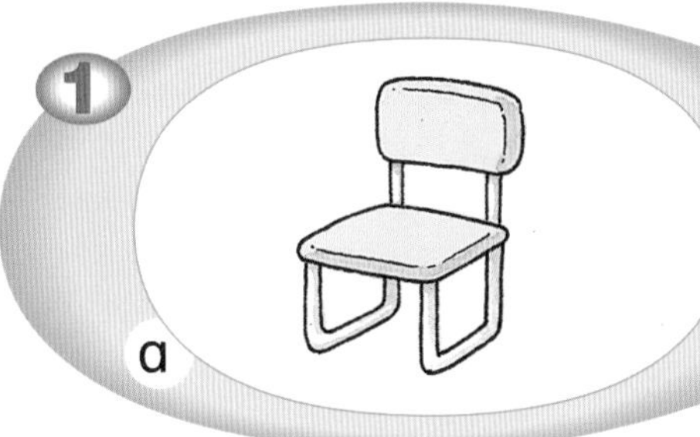
a

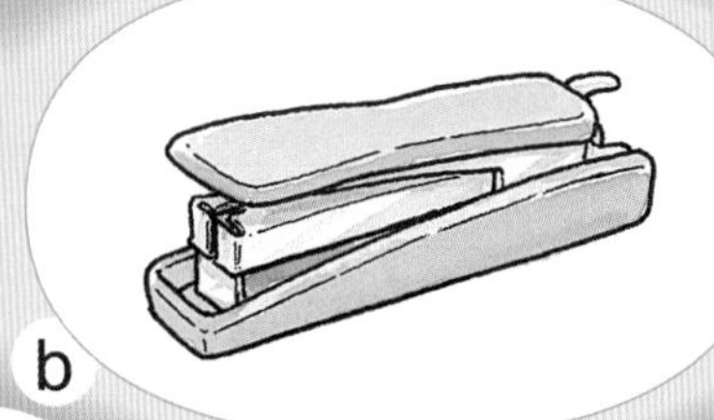
b

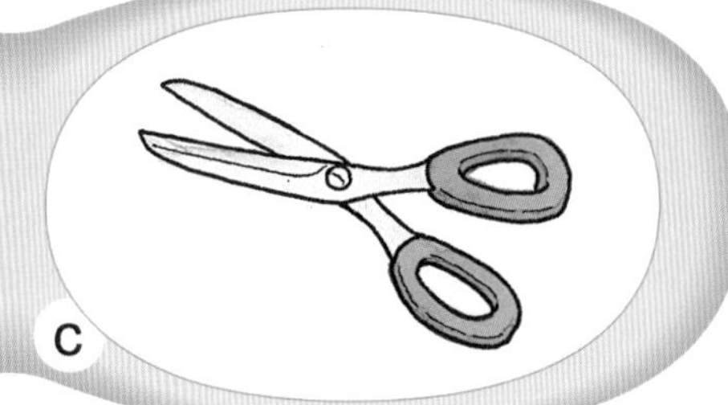
c

2

a

b

c

3

Ketnaro
a

Ktentrao
b

Kentaro
c

4

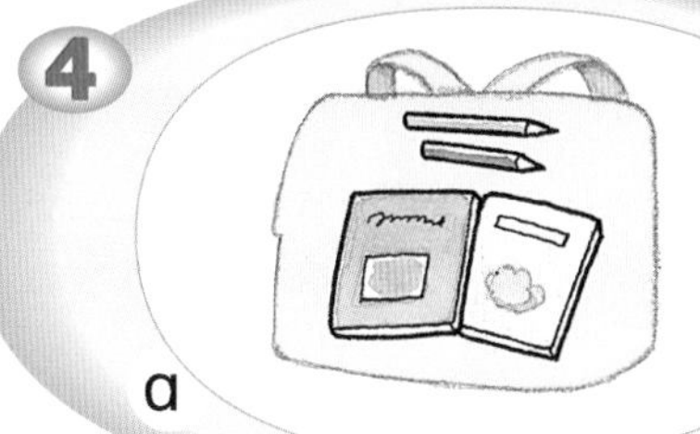
a

b

c

CD 30

ABCDEFGHIJKLMNOPQRSTUVWXYZ

A a

/ Λ A

c a

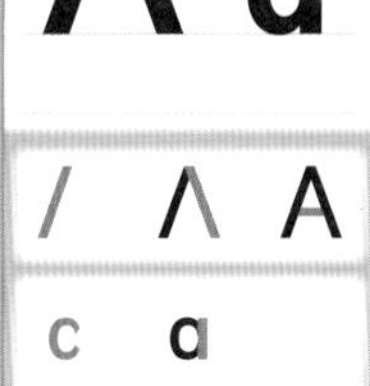

B b

l P B

l b

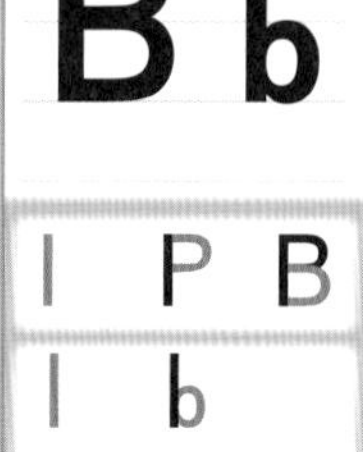

C c

C

c

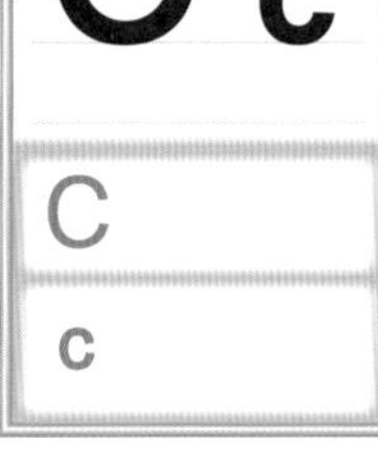

D d

l D

c d

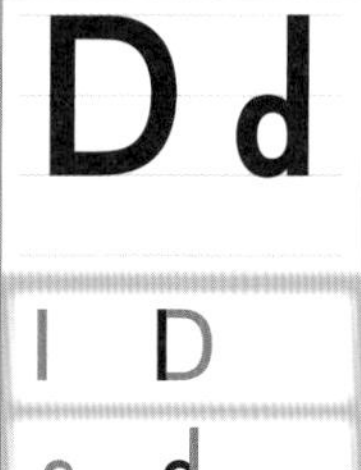

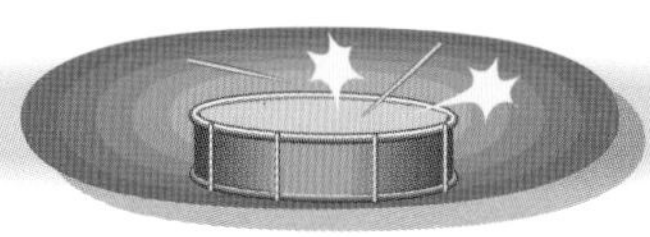

CD 31

What's this? What's this? What's this in English?

A stapler.

Once more, please.

A stapler.

Louder, please.

A stapler. A stapler. A STAPLER!

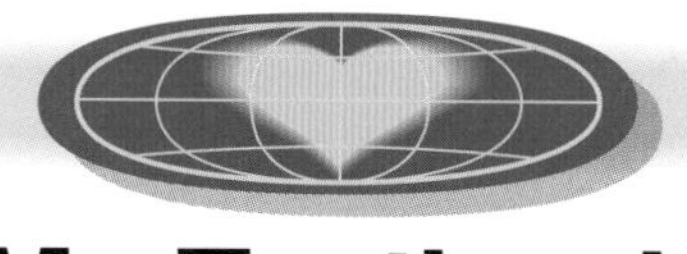

My Textbook

CD 80

This is my textbook.
I like social studies.

This is my textbook.
I like Spanish.

This is my textbook.
I like Thai language.

This is my textbook.
I like math.

This is my textbook.

I like

On the School Ground

CD 33→34
Let's play soccer.
Yes, let's.

CD 32 vocabulary song

walk hop skip (dance swim fly)

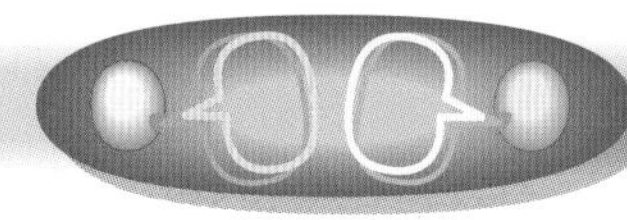

CD 35

 May we go out to play?

 Sure.

 Go! Run! Kick the ball!

 Go! Don't stop!
Get the ball.

CD 36

Words

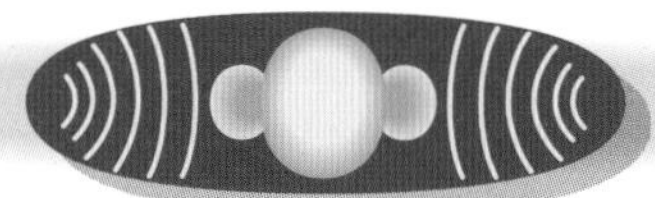

1

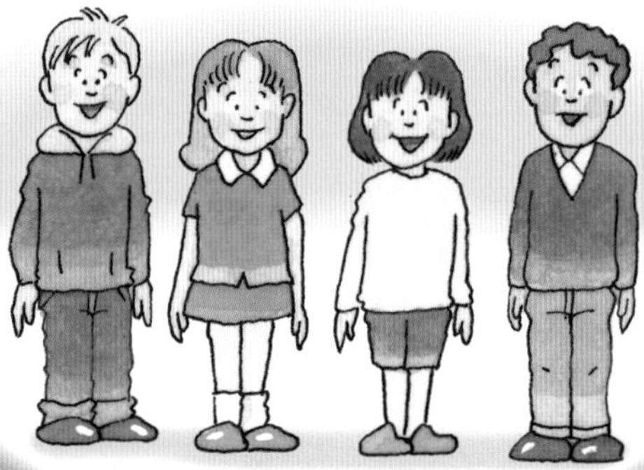

a b c

2

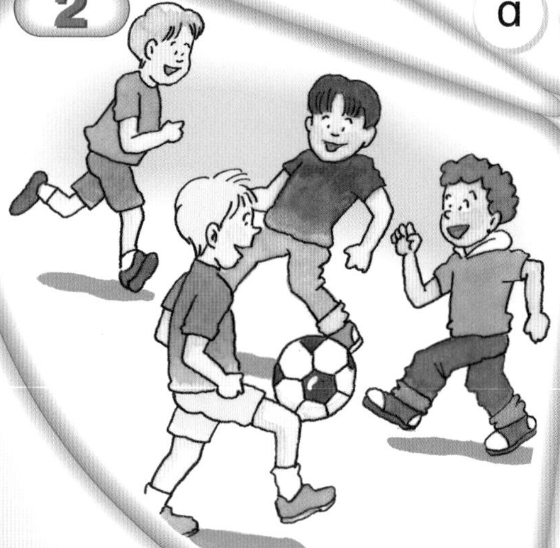

a b c

3

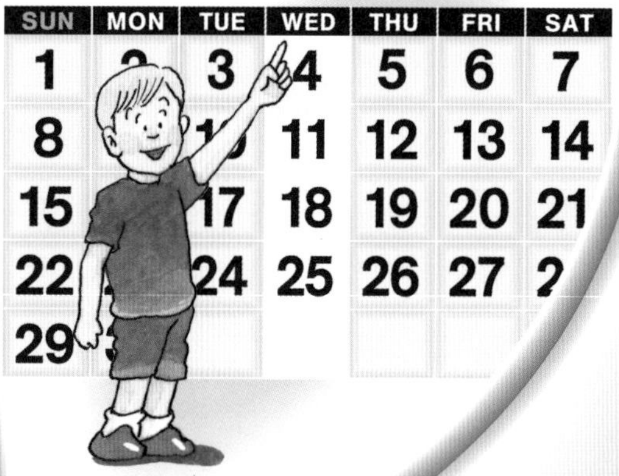

SUN MON TUE WED THU FRI SAT
1 3 4 5 6 7
8 11 12 13 14
15 17 18 19 20 21
22 24 25 26 27
29

a b c

CD 37

ABCDEFGHIJKLMNOPQRSTUVWXYZ

E e

I Γ F E

e

F f

I Γ F

ſ f

G g

C G

c g

H h

I ⊢ H

l h

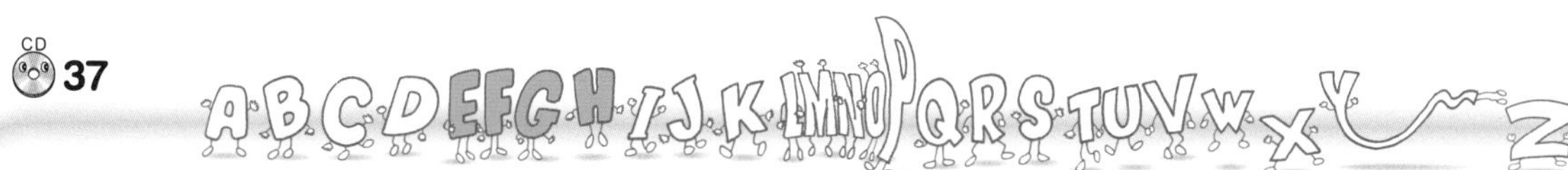

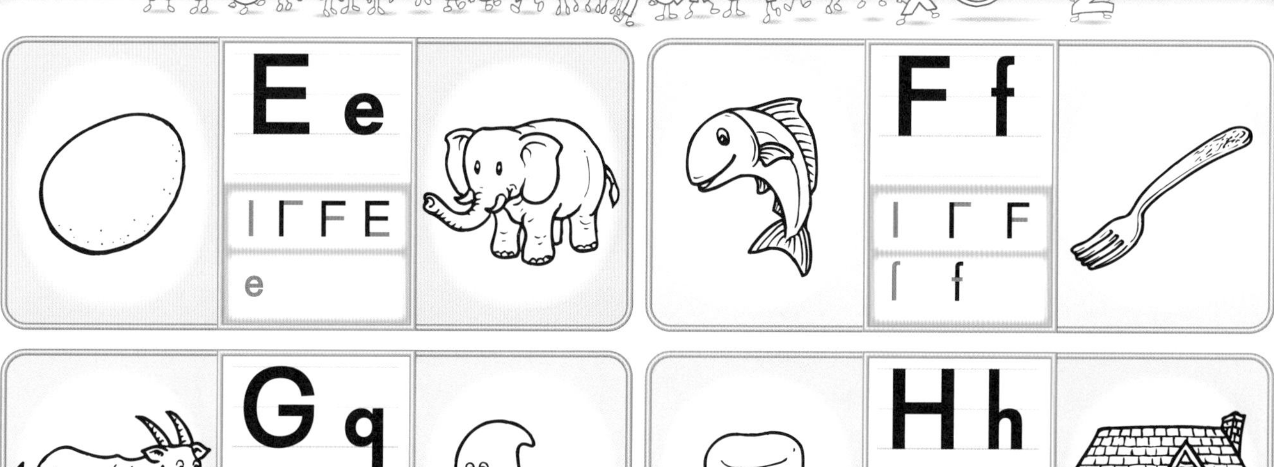

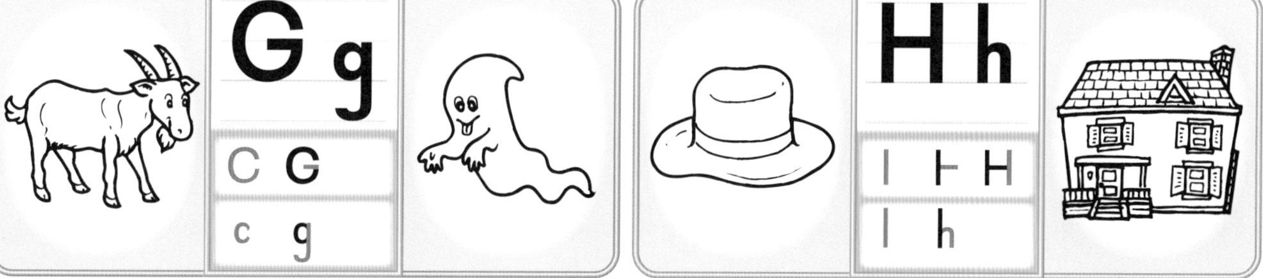

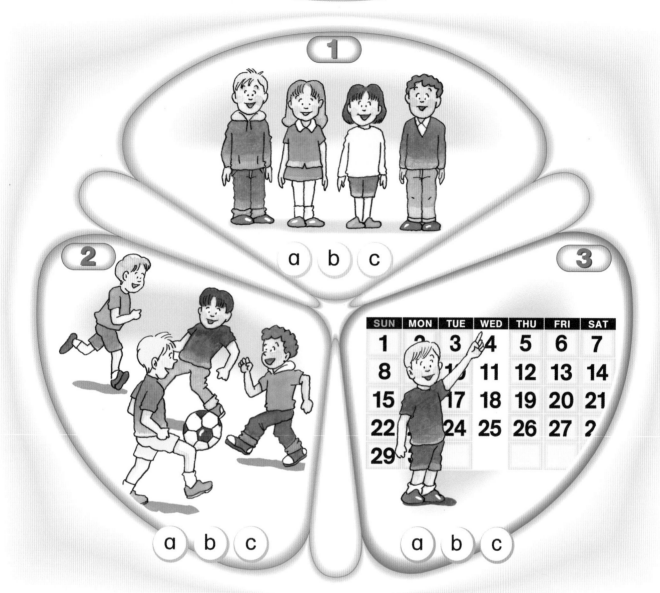

Break time. Are you ready?

Let's go out.

Let's run. Let's climb. Let's play dodgeball.

Break time. Are you ready?

Let's go out.

My House

CD 81

This is my house.
I live in Vancouver, Canada.

This is my house.
I live in Guadalajara, Mexico.

This is my house.
I live in Bangkok, Thailand.

This is my house (apartment).
I live in Shanghai, China.

This is my house.

I live in

At the School Cafeteria

40→41
Are you hungry?
Yes, I am. I'm starving.
Me, too.
39
vocabulary song
happy
angry
brave
sad
merry
hungry
tired

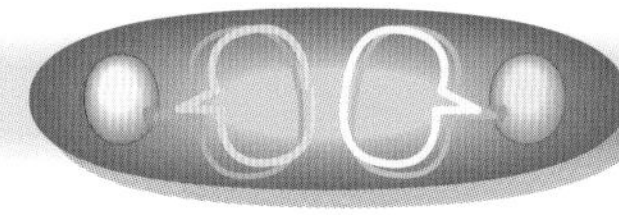

CD 42

 Two apples, please.

 OK. Here you are.

 Excuse me.

 Wait a minute.
Get in line.

 Oh, I'm sorry.

CD 43

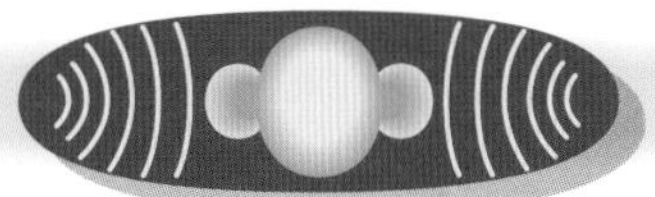

1

a

b

c

a

b

c

a

b

c

a

b

c

CD 44

ABCDEFGHIJKLMNOPQRSTUVWXYZ

I i

I I I

i i

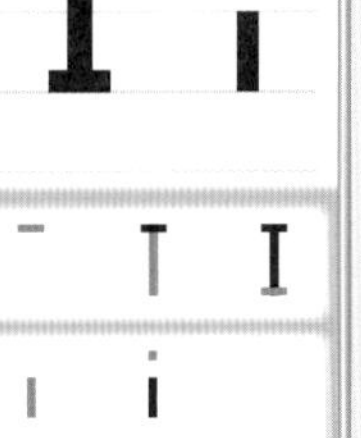

J j

J

j j

K k

I K K

I k k

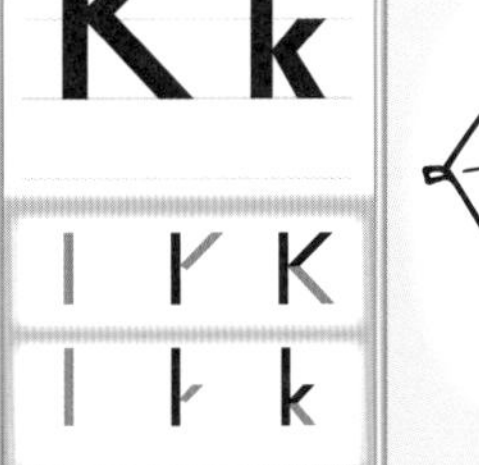

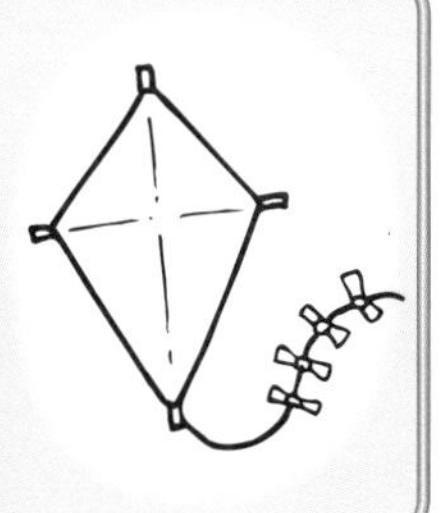

L l

L

l

Let's eat lunch. Yum, yum, yum.

Wash your hands and get a tray.

A fork, a knife, a glass and a plate.

I like pizza, salad and milk.

Let's eat lunch. Yum, yum, yum.

My Lunch

CD 82

This is my lunch.
I like pizza.

This is my lunch.
I like tortillas, frijoles and salsa.

This is my lunch.
I like fried curry shrimp and fried chicken.

This is my lunch.
I like spinach, boiled shrimp and boiled duck.

abc

This is my lunch.

I like

At the School Physical

E
SNT
RQPHF
LMPODAC
CD 47→48
Can you see this letter?
Yes, I can. It's a "D".
CD 46
vocabulary song
head
shoulders
knees
toes
eyes
ears
mouth
nose

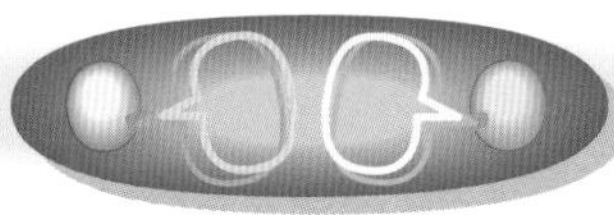

CD 49

How tall are you?

I'm 140cm tall.

How tall are you?

I'm 132cm tall.

How much do you weigh?

It's a secret!

CD 50

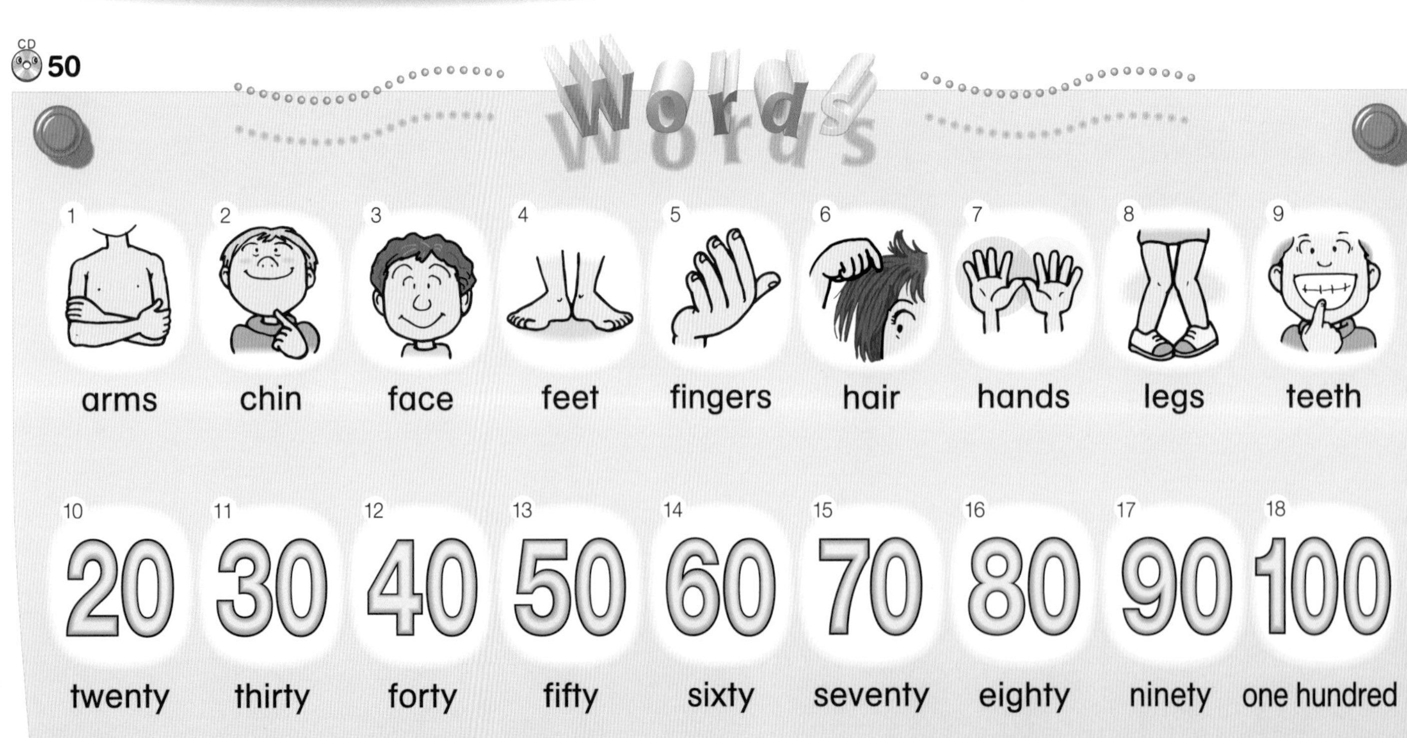

1

113cm

a b c

2

I weigh 30kg.

a b c

3

a b c

CD 51

ABCDEFGHIJKLMNOPQRSTUVWXYZ

	Mm M m	
	Nn N n	
	Oo O o	
	Pp P p	

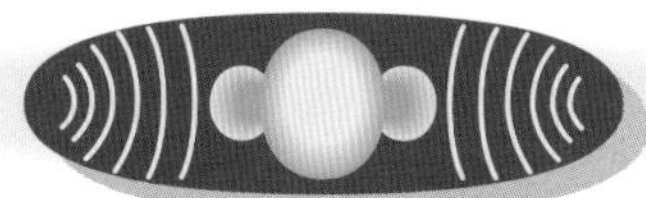

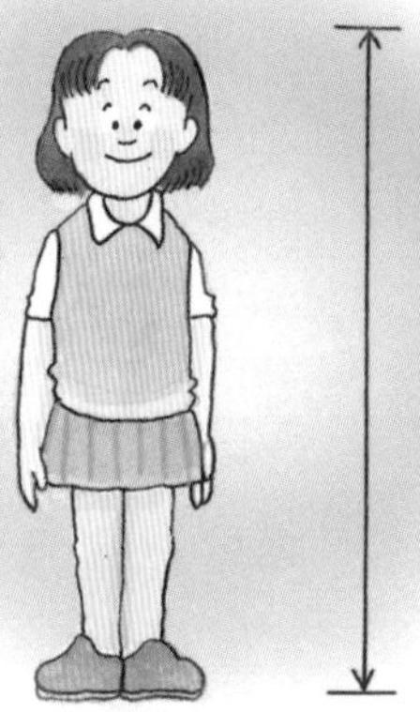

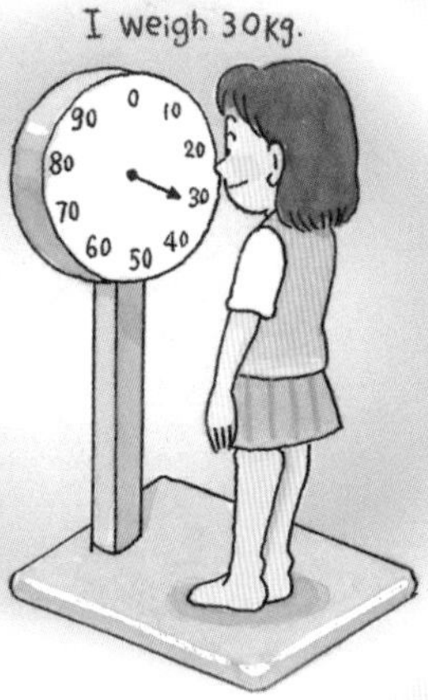

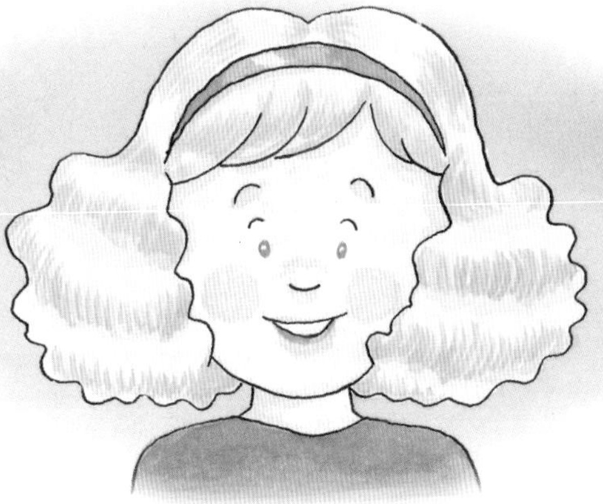

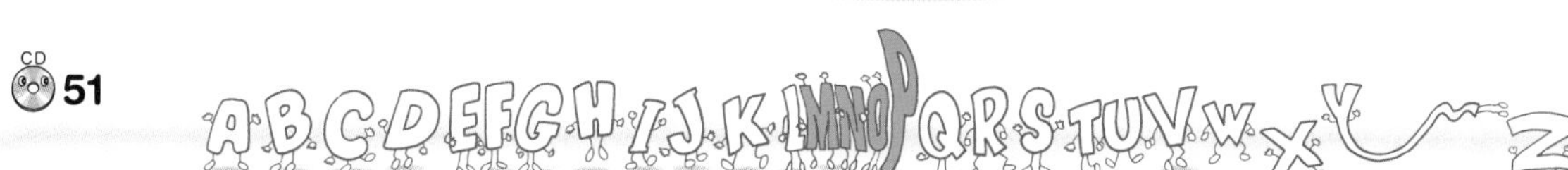

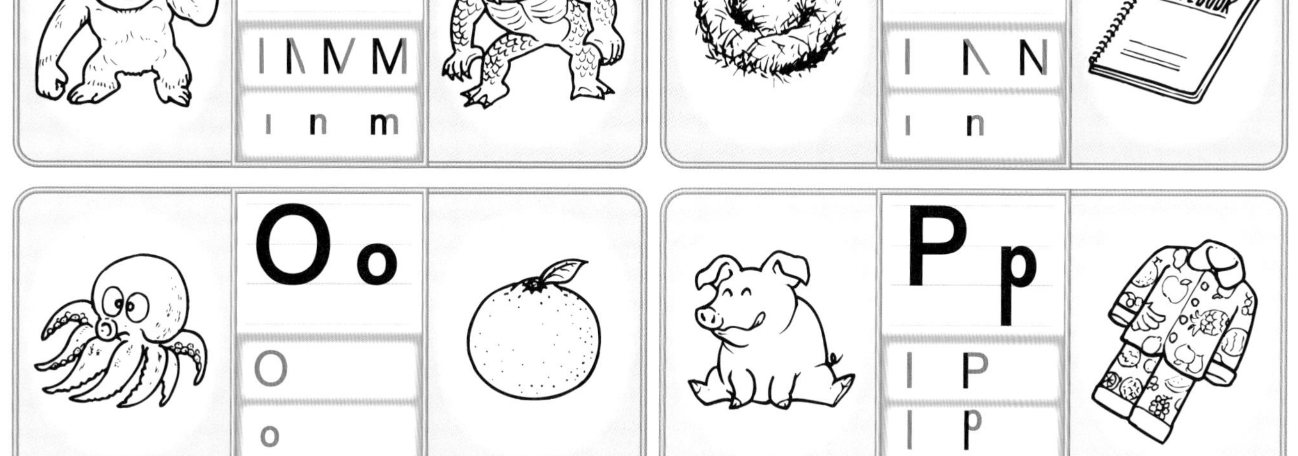

With my eyes, I can see.

With my ears, I can hear.

With my nose, I can smell.

With my mouth, I can talk.

With my legs, I can walk.

And with your love,

what can you do?

My Treasures

CD 83

These are my treasures.
They are ice skates.

This is my treasure.
It is Superman.

This is my treasure.
It is a beaver.

These are my treasures.
They are a bear and a mouse.

This is my treasure.

It is

In the School Garden

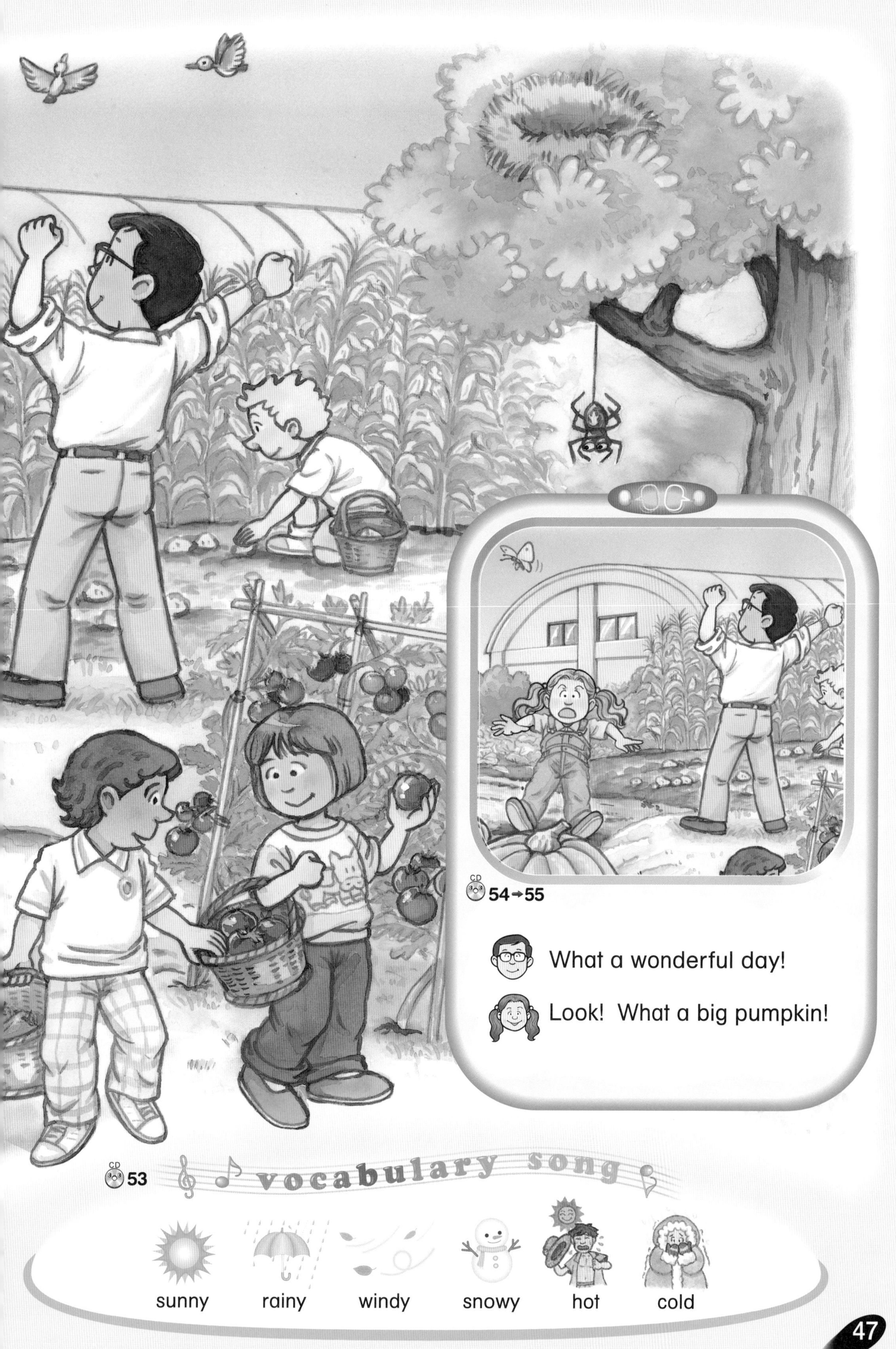
CD 54→55
What a wonderful day!
Look! What a big pumpkin!
CD 53
vocabulary song
sunny
rainy
windy
snowy
hot
cold

56

How many tomatoes do you have in your basket?

I have nine tomatoes.

Please come and help me!

I'm coming.

CD 57

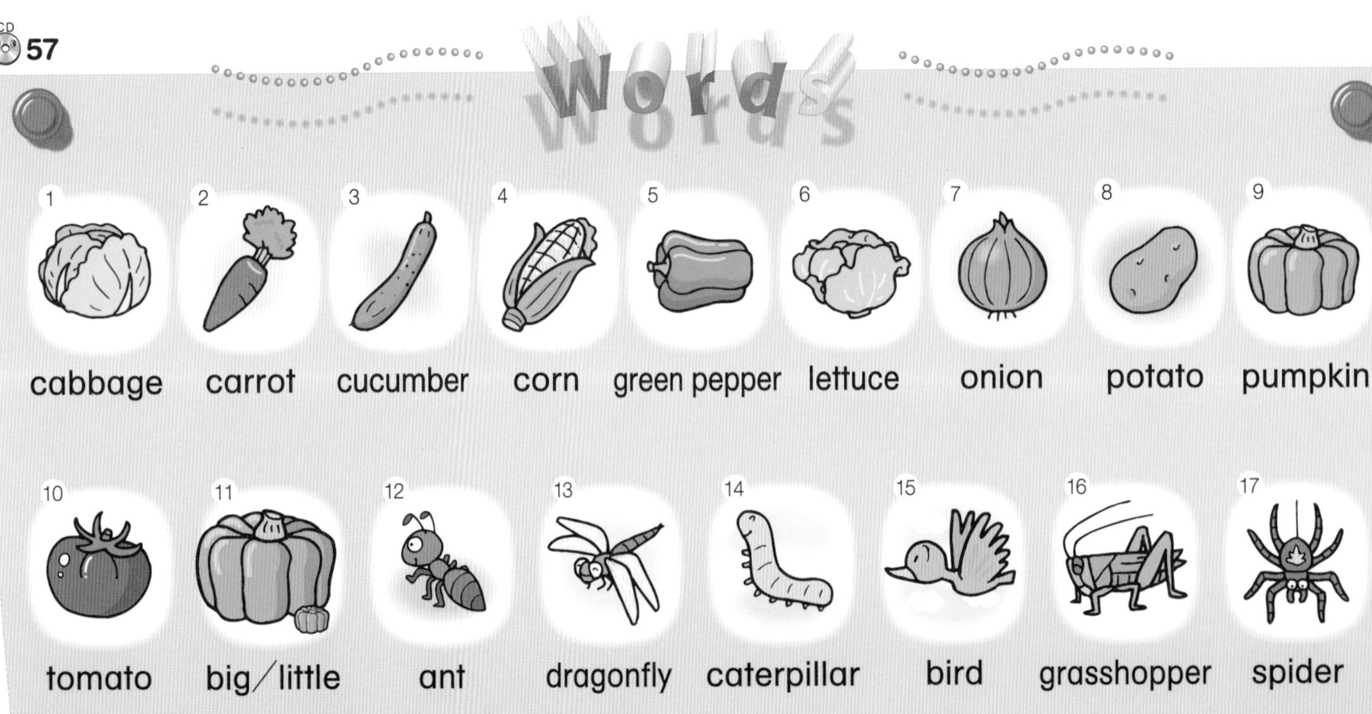

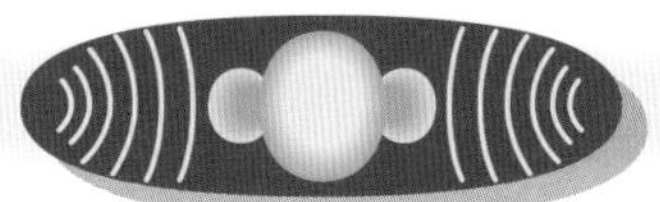

1

a

b

c

2

a

b

c

3

a

b

c

4

a

b

c

58

ABCDEFGHIJKLMNOPQRSTUVWXYZ

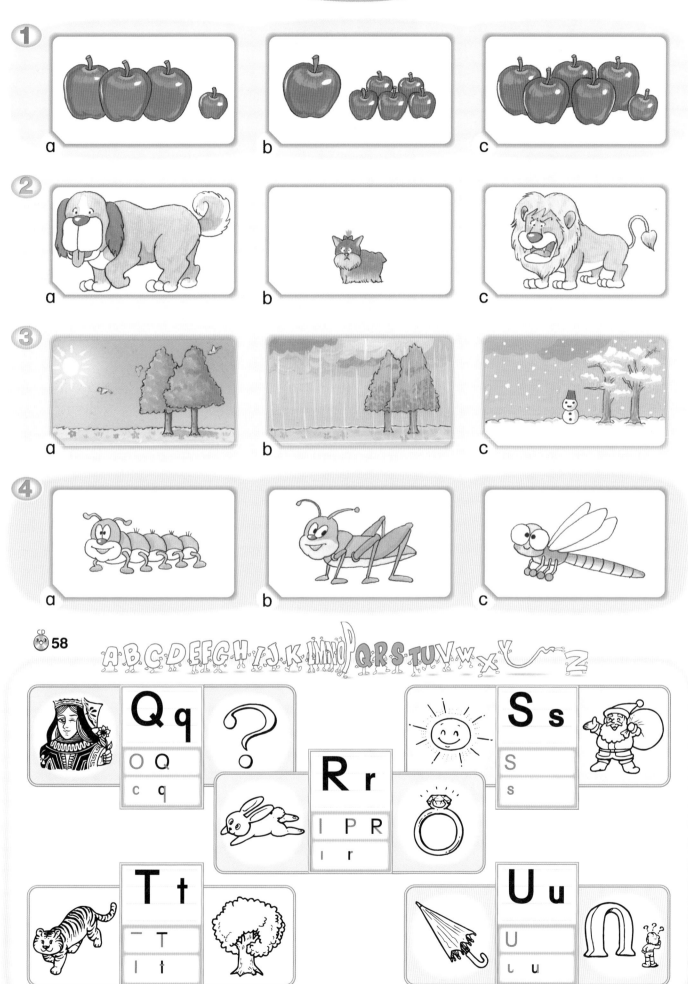

Q q

O Q

c q

R r

I P R

ı r

S s

S

s

T t

‾ T

I t

U u

U

ι u

CD 59

It's sunny today.

Open the window. Feel the sun.

It's sunny today.

It's rainy today.

Open the window. Feel the rain.

It's rainy today.

It's windy today.

Open the window. Feel the wind.

It's windy today.

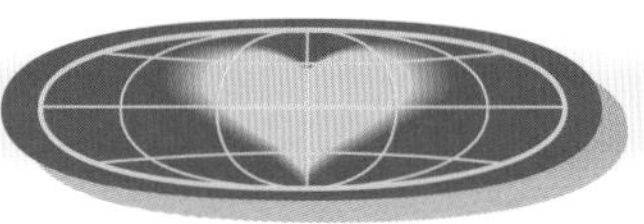

CD 84

My Favorite Animals

I want to meet a reindeer
walking on the snow.
A big reindeer walking in Finland.

I want to meet a toucan
flying in the rain forest.
A colorful toucan flying in the sky.

I want to meet a tiger
sleeping in the woods.
A strong tiger sleeping in India.

I want to meet a killer whale
swimming in the ocean.
A beautiful killer whale jumping
out of the water.

I want to meet

On Sunday with My Family

CD 61→62

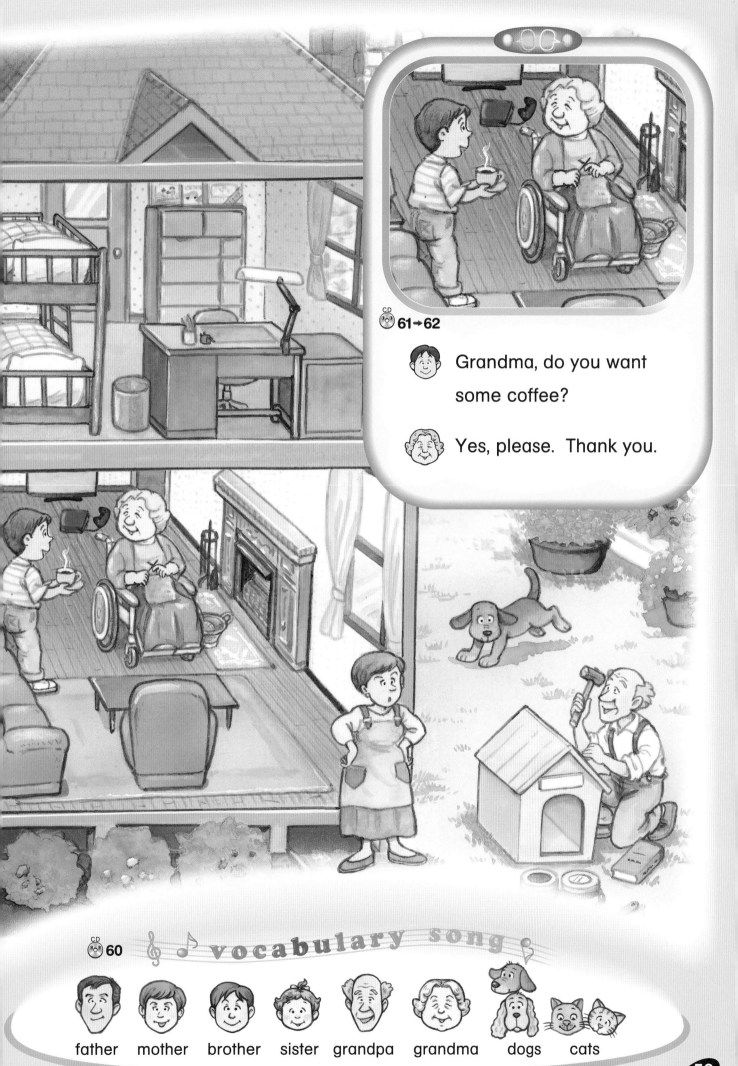

Grandma, do you want some coffee?

Yes, please. Thank you.

CD 60 vocabulary song

father

mother

brother

sister

grandpa

grandma

dogs

cats

CD 63

Dad, where are you?

I'm in the garage.

Have you finished?

Almost.

CD 64

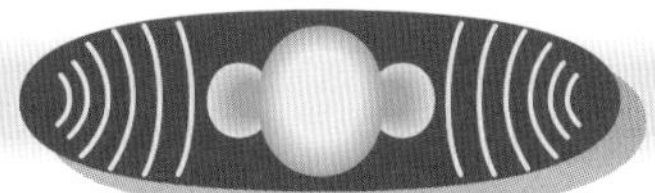

a

b

c

a

b

c

a

b

c

a

b

c

CD 65

A B C D E F G H I J K L M N O P Q R S T U V W X Y Z

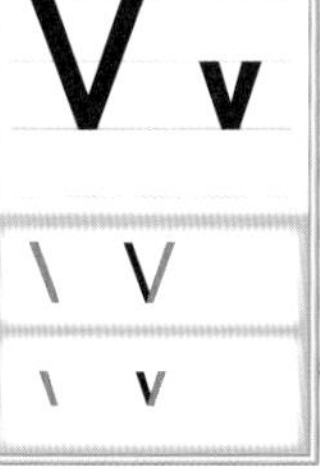

V v

W w

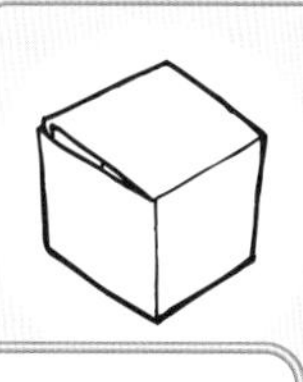
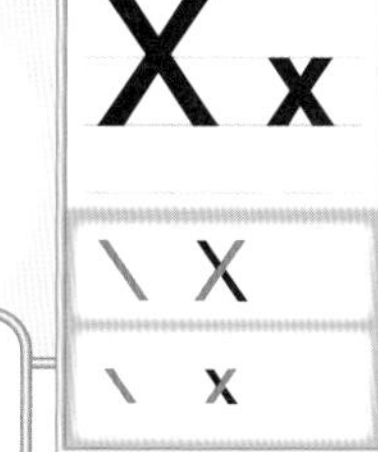

X x

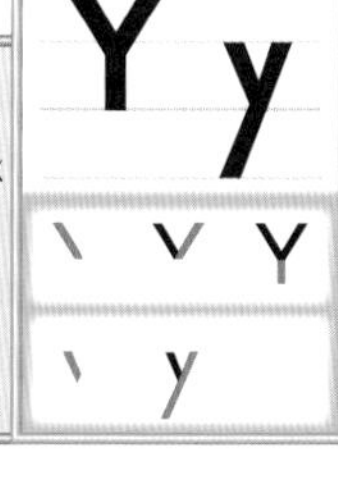

Y y

Z z

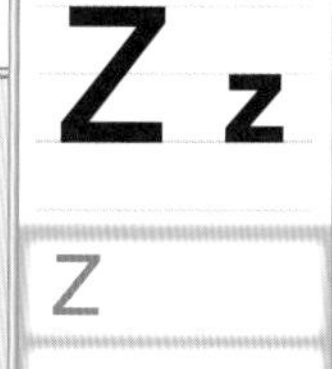

CD 66

Where's Dad?

He's in the garage.

What's he doing?

Washing his car.

Where's Mom?

She's in the kitchen.

What's she doing?

Making our lunch.

Where's grandpa?

He's in the yard.

What's he doing?

Taking a nap, taking a nap with a big pillow.

My Family

CD 85

This is my family.
My mother, my father,
my brother, and my dog.

This is my family.
My mother, my father, my sisters,
and my brother. And my parrot.

This is my family.
My mother, my father,
and my sisters.

This is my family.
My mother and my father.

This is my family.

At the Supermarket

CD 67 vocabulary song

A HAPPY NEW YEAR
January
St.Valentine's Day
February
March
April
May
June
July
August

CD 68→69

We need eggs, milk, bread and sugar.

Let's buy some strawberries.

OK.

September October November December

CD 70

 This watermelon looks good.

 Let's buy one.

 How much is it?

 Twenty dollars, please.

CD 71

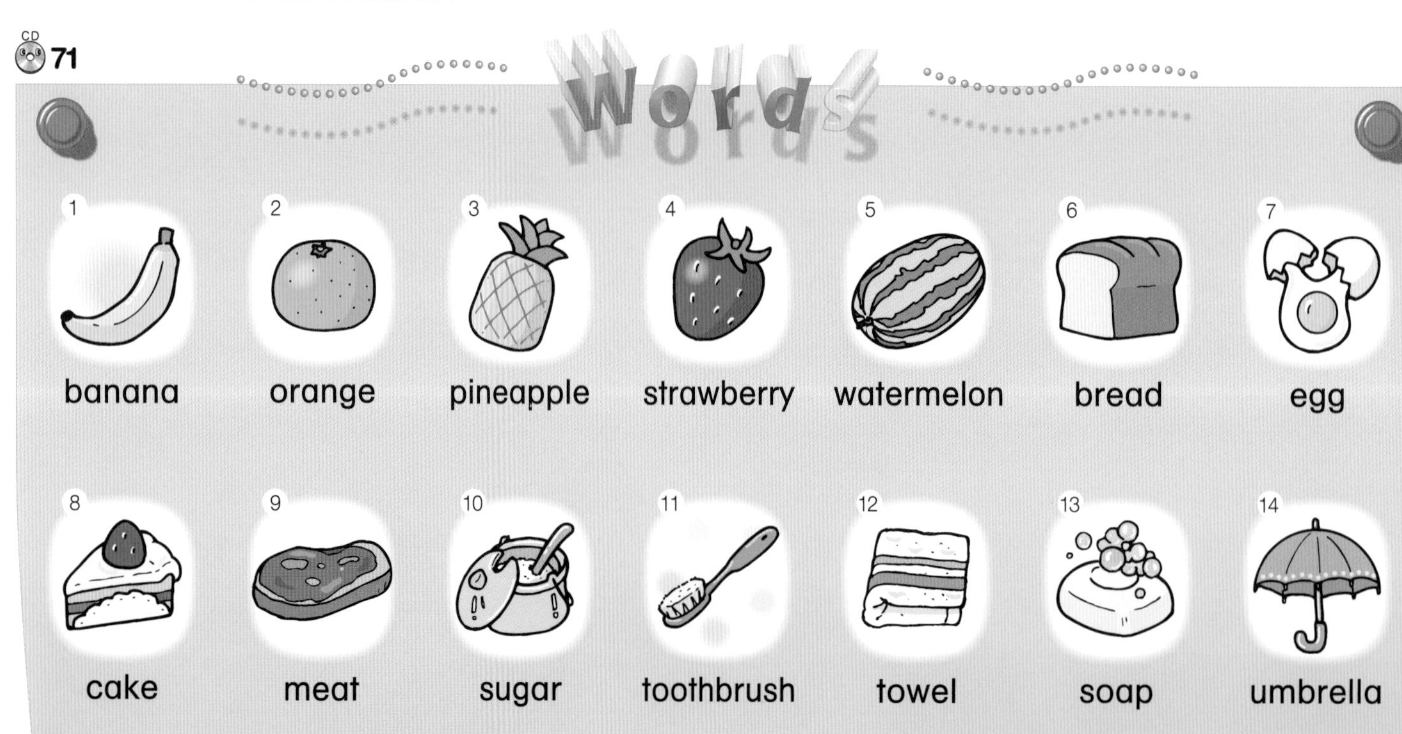

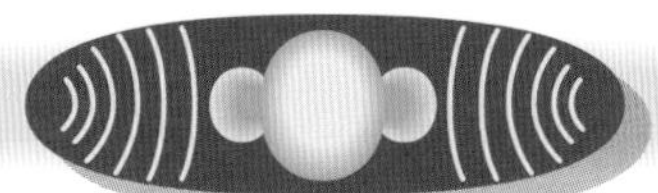

30yen each

100yen each

50yen each

120yen each

300yen each

1 yen

3 yen

2 yen

4 yen

CD 73

A B C D E F G H I J K L M N O P Q R S T U V W X Y Z

① c t

② m p

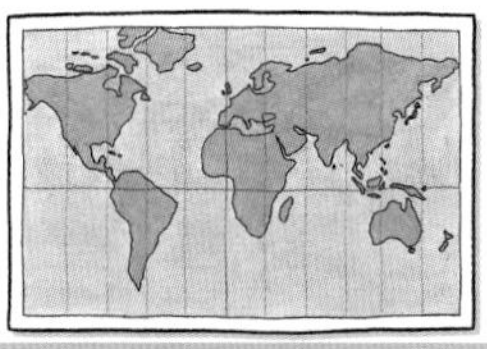

③ b d

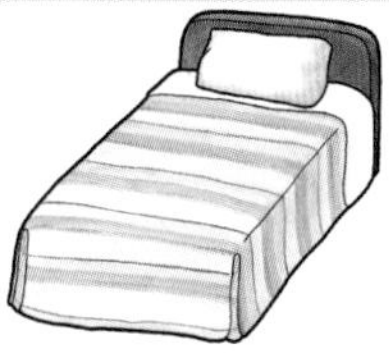

④ n t

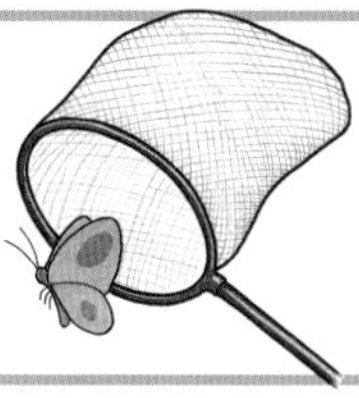

⑤ p g

⑥ l p

⑦ b x

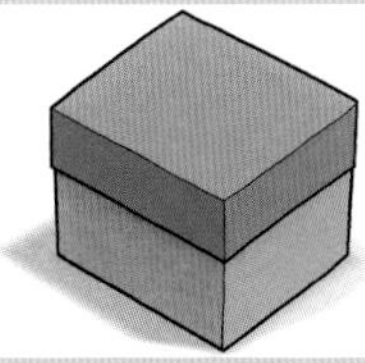

⑧ m p

⑨ s n

⑩ c p

Let's take a look. In the market, what can you see?

I can see carrots. What can you see?

I can see eggs.   What can you see?

Let's take a look. In the zoo, what can you see?

I can see monkeys. What can you see?

I can see lions.   What can you see?

Let's take a look. In the school, what can you see?

I can see a blackboard. What can you see?

I can see a teacher.   What can you see?

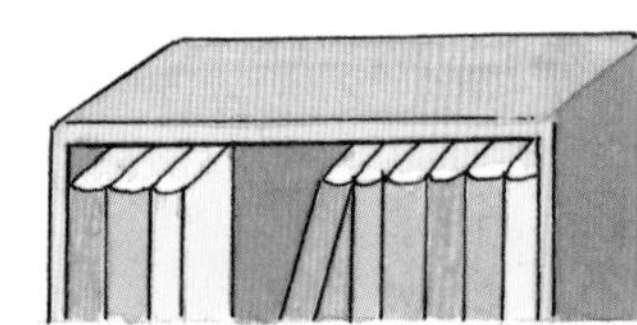

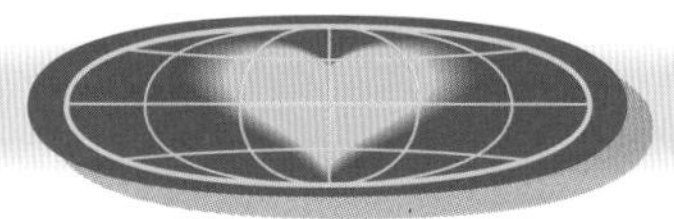

CD 86

More about Myself

My name is Kaetlyn. My birthday is December 25th.

I like green. I like playing the piano.
I am good at skating.
I want to be a piano teacher.

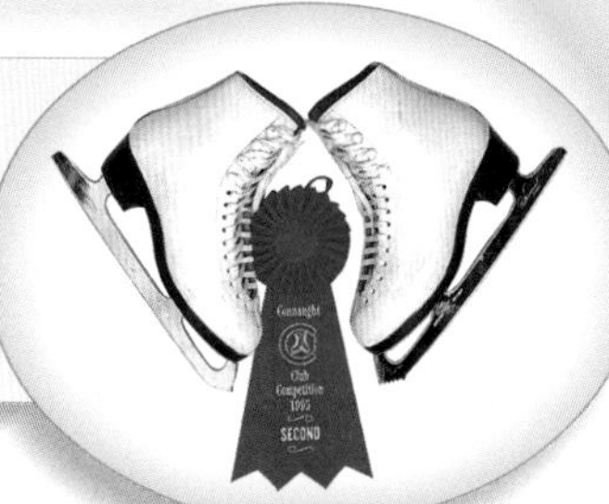

My name is Eric. My birthday is July 9th.

I like blue. I like playing soccer.
My favorite food is tacos.
I want to be a police officer.

My name is Kanjana. My birthday is October 5th.

I like pink. I like playing volleyball.
My father works at this market.
I want to be a teacher.

My name is Tian. My birthday is September 5th.

I like green. I like playing soccer.
She is my teacher.
I want to be a doctor.

自分のことをどれだけ言えるかな？

Tell us more about you!

CD 74→75

Song Three-letter words: The Vowel song

Little a, little a, [æ] [æ] [æ], little a, little a, [æ] [æ] [æ],
Tell me words with a in the middle, bat, cap, cat, fan, hat.

a

bat	cap	cat	fan	hat

Little e, little e, [e] [e] [e], little e, little e, [e] [e] [e],
Tell me words with e in the middle, bed, hen, jet, net, pen.

e

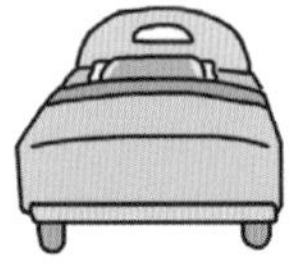				
bed	hen	jet	net	pen

Little i, little i, [i] [i] [i], little i, little i, [i] [i] [i],
Tell me words with i in the middle, fin, lip, pig, pin, six.

fin	lip	pig	pin	six

Little o, little o, [ɔ] [ɔ] [ɔ], little o, little o, [ɔ] [ɔ] [ɔ],
Tell me words with o in the middle, box, dog, fox, hop, mop.

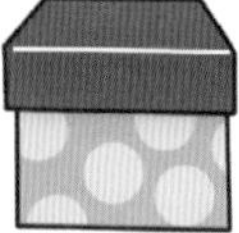				
box	dog	fox	hop	mop

Little u, little u, [ʌ] [ʌ] [ʌ], little u, little u, [ʌ] [ʌ] [ʌ],
Tell me words with u in the middle, bug, bun, bus, cup, gun.

bug	bun	bus	cup	gun

Words by Mikiko Nakamoto/ Composed by Akiko Arai

Let's read!

a sad cat in a bag

a big red pen

hot milk in a pot

a fat pig on a bus

a mop on a map

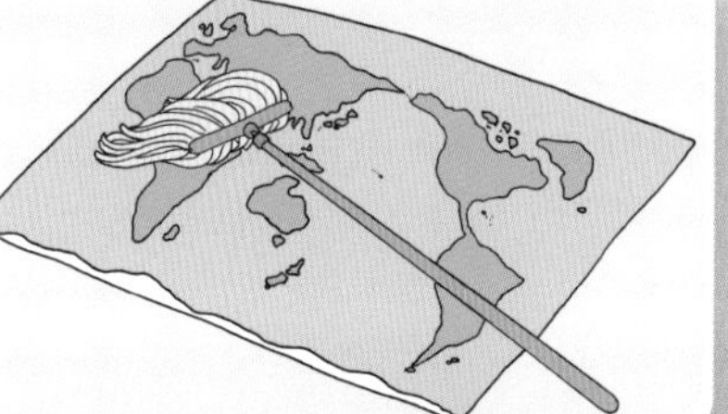

a bug in a cup

words words words

CD 9→87 Unit 1 B p.6 vocabulary song

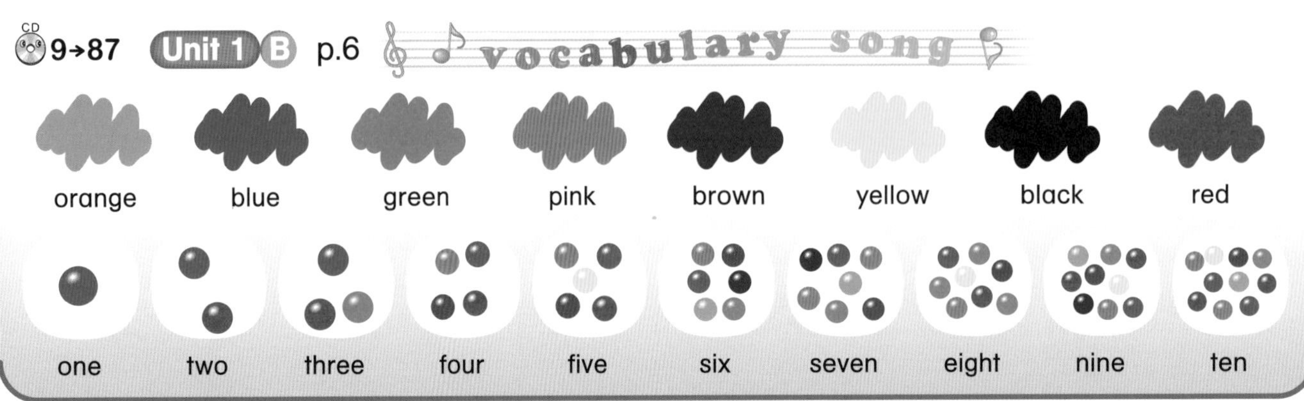

orange blue green pink brown yellow black red

one two three four five six seven eight nine ten

CD 12→88 Unit 2 A p.11

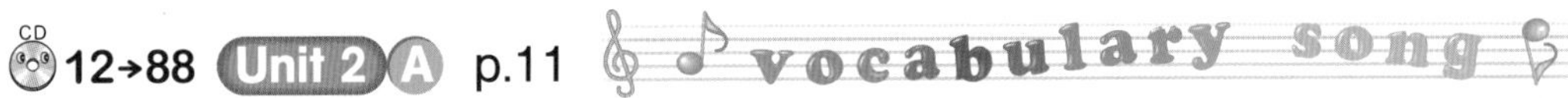

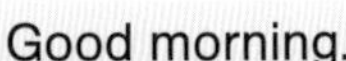

Good morning.

Good afternoon.

Good evening.

CD 16 Unit 2 B p.12

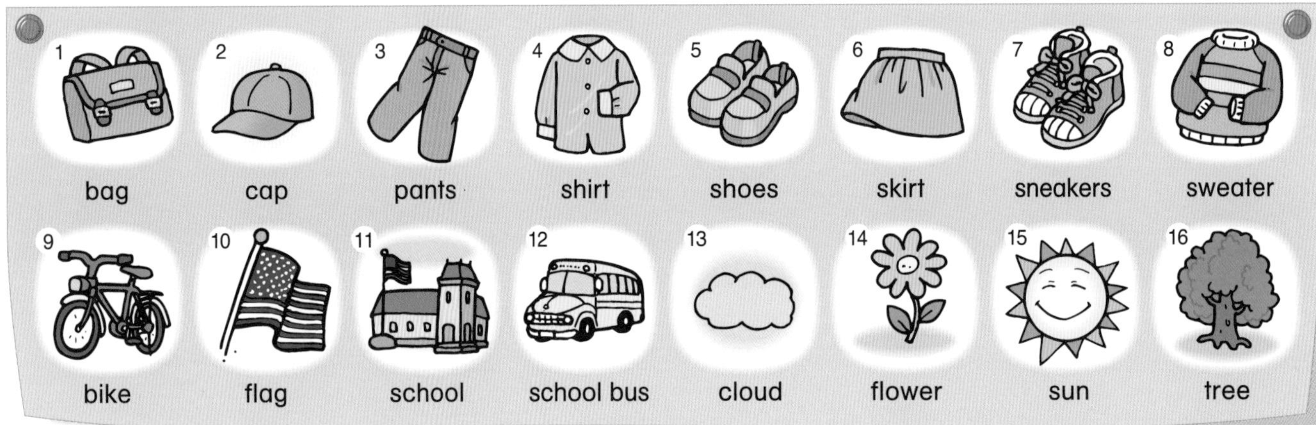

1 bag 2 cap 3 pants 4 shirt 5 shoes 6 skirt 7 sneakers 8 sweater

9 bike 10 flag 11 school 12 school bus 13 cloud 14 flower 15 sun 16 tree

CD 19→89 Unit 3 A pp.16-17

Hello.

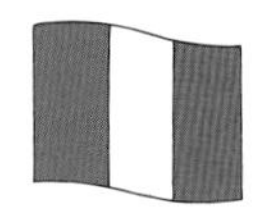
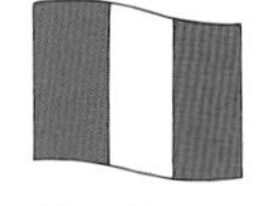

Bonjour.

你好

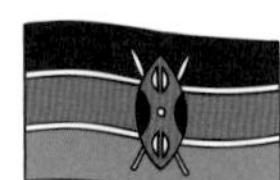

Hujambo.

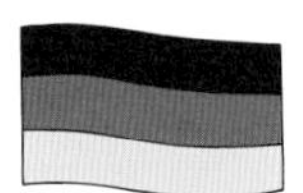

Guten Tag.

Buenos días.

안녕하십니까?

สวัสดี(ค่ะ)

नमस्ते

こんにちは

CD 25→90 Unit 4 A p.23 vocabulary song

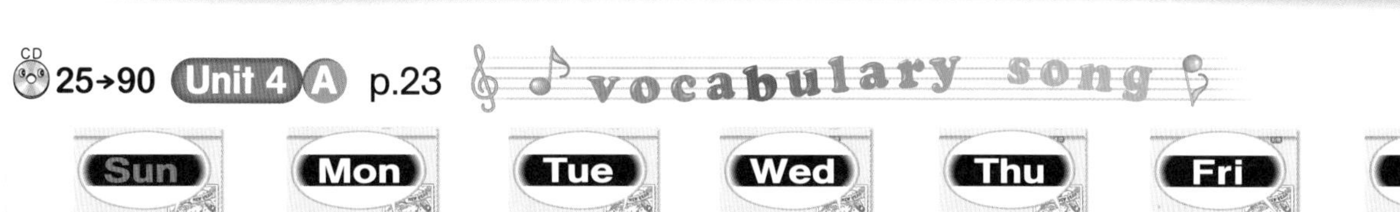

Sunday Monday Tuesday Wednesday Thursday Friday Saturday

CD 29 Unit 4 B p.24 Words

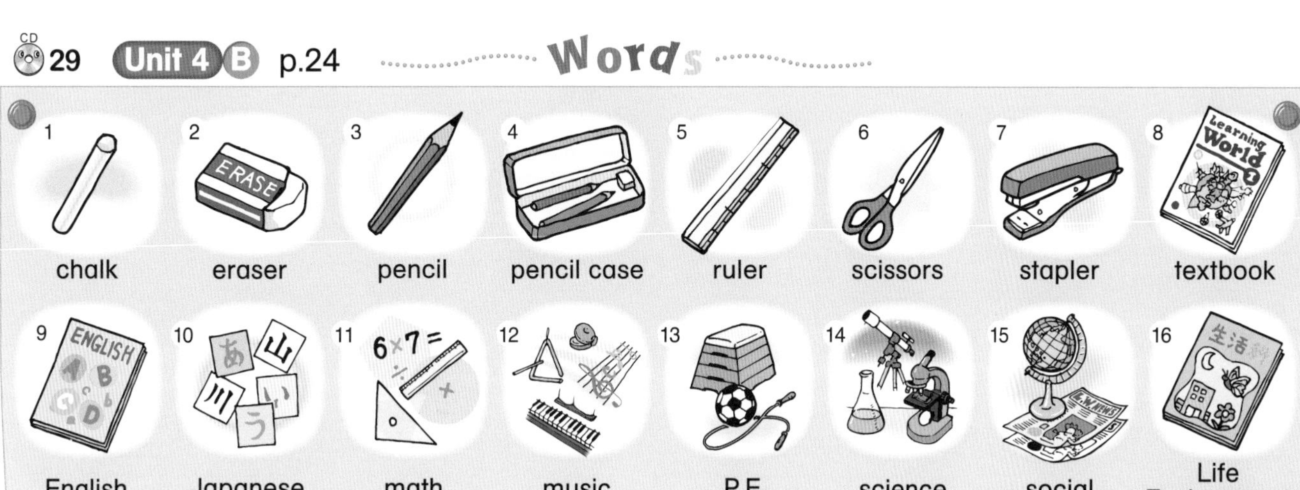

CD 32→91 Unit 5 A p.29 vocabulary song

walk hop skip (dance swim fly)

CD 36 Unit 5 B p.30 Words

CD 39→92 Unit 6 A p.35 vocabulary song

happy

angry

brave

sad

merry

hungry

tired

CD 43 Unit 6 B p.36 Words

1 
apple

2 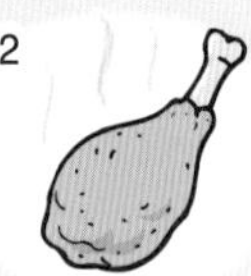
fried chicken

3 
hamburger

4 

milk

5 
orange juice

6 
pizza

7 
salad

8 
sandwich

9 
spaghetti

10 
fork

11 
glass

12 
knife

13 
plate

14 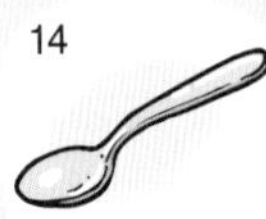
spoon

15 
table

16 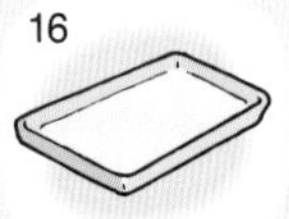
tray

CD 46→93 Unit 7 A p.41 vocabulary song

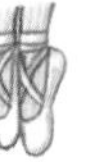

head

shoulders

knees

toes

eyes

ears

mouth

nose

CD 50 Unit 7 B p.42 Words

1 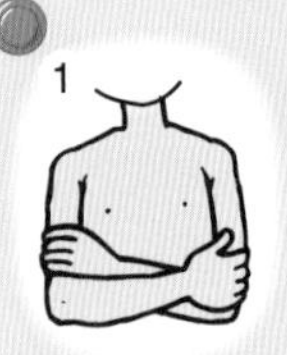
arms

2 
chin

3 
face

4 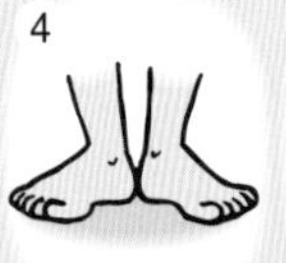
feet

5 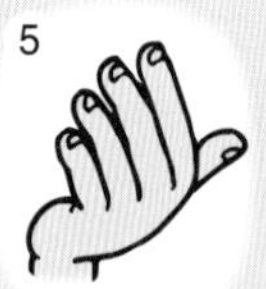
fingers

6 
hair

7 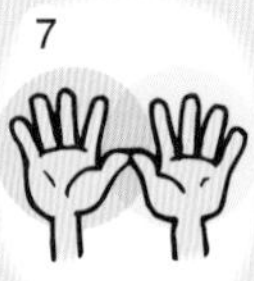
hands

8 
legs

9 
teeth

10 
20
twenty

11 
30
thirty

12 
40
forty

13 50
fifty

14 60
sixty

15 70
seventy

16 80
eighty

17 90
ninety

18 100
one hundred

CD 53→94 Unit 8 A p.47 vocabulary song

sunny

rainy

windy

snowy

hot

cold

CD
57
Unit 8 B
p.48
Words

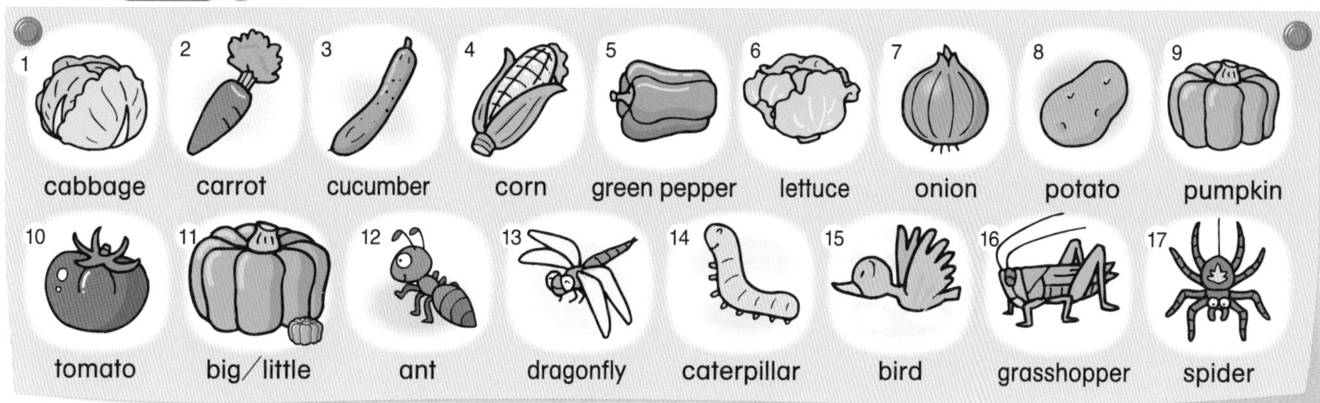

1 cabbage
2 carrot
3 cucumber
4 corn
5 green pepper
6 lettuce
7 onion
8 potato
9 pumpkin
10 tomato
11 big/little
12 ant
13 dragonfly
14 caterpillar
15 bird
16 grasshopper
17 spider

CD
60→95
Unit 9 A
p.53
vocabulary song

father
mother
brother
sister
grandpa
grandma
dogs
cats

CD
64
Unit 9 B
p.54
Words
1 bed
2 wheelchair
3 curtain
4 sofa
5 telephone
6 television
7 video game
8 bathtub
9 bathroom
10 bedroom
11 living room
12 kitchen
13 garage
14 garden
15 chimney
16 roof

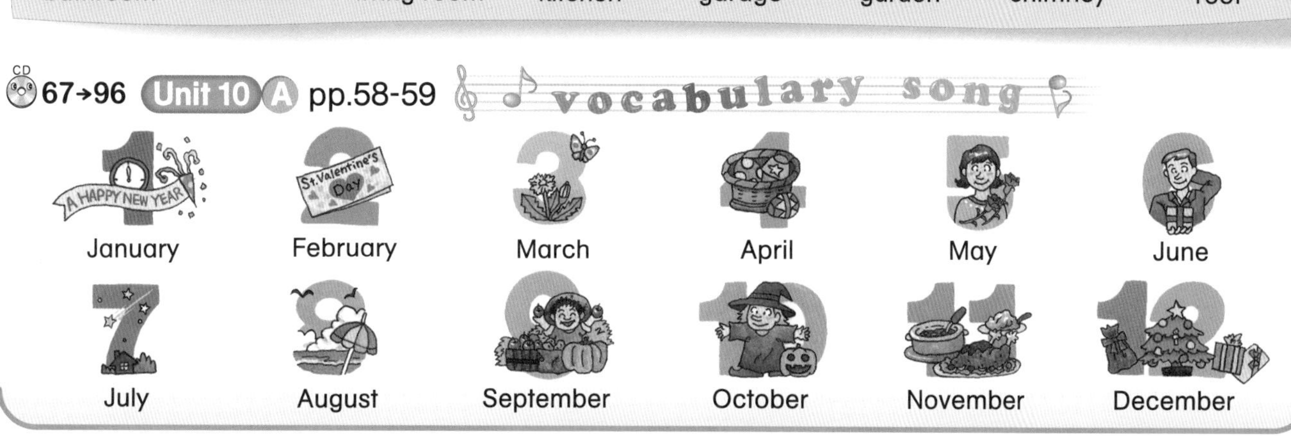

CD
67→96
Unit 10 A
pp.58-59
vocabulary song
A HAPPY NEW YEAR
January
St. Valentine's Day
February
March
April
May
June
July
August
September
October
November
December

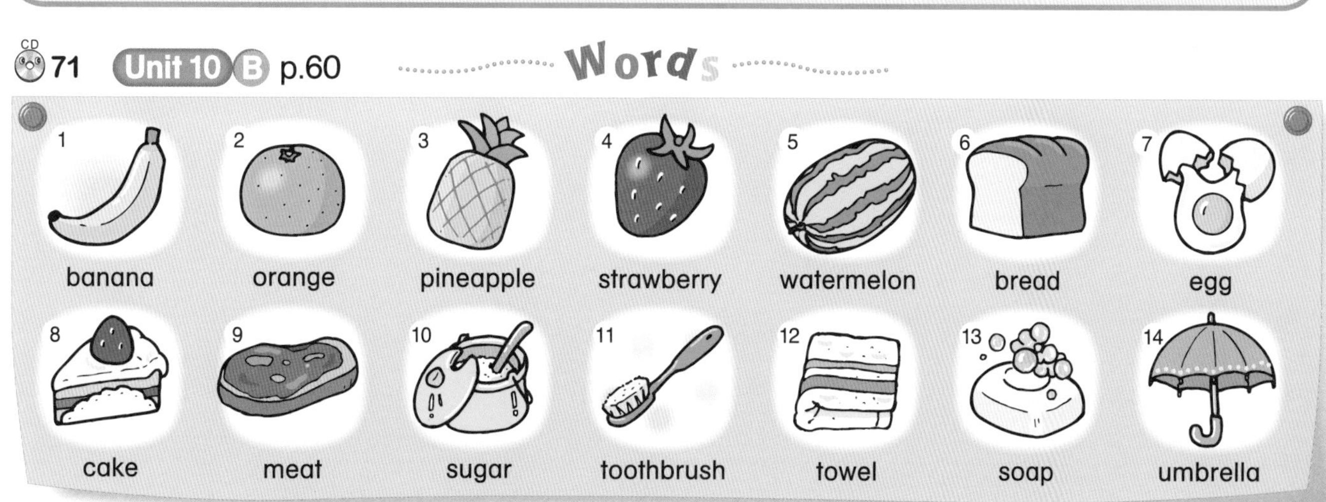

CD
71
Unit 10 B
p.60
Words
1 banana
2 orange
3 pineapple
4 strawberry
5 watermelon
6 bread
7 egg
8 cake
9 meat
10 sugar
11 toothbrush
12 towel
13 soap
14 umbrella

Unit	A		B
	Dialogues	Vocabulary Songs	Dialogues
1 Nice to Meet You はじめまして	●My name is Kaetlyn. ●I am ... years old. ●I'm from Canada.	♪ **The Color and Number song** (p.6)	●What's your name? My name is... ●How old are you? I'm ten years old. ●Where do you live? I live in Canada.
2 On the Way to School 学校に行く途中で	●Good morning, Mr. Takahashi. ●How are you, Kaetlyn? ●I'm fine.	♪ **The Greeting song** Good morning, Good afternoon, Good evening.	●How do you come to school? By bus. ●Good-bye. See you later.
3 In the Classroom 学校のクラスルームで 新入生紹介	●This is our new friend. Her name is Yuko Treadway. ●She is from Japan. ●My name is.... ●Nice to meet you.	♪ **Hello song** Hello, Bonjour, Ni hao, Hujambo, Guten Tag, Buenos dias, Annoyong hasipnikka, Sawas dee, Namastee, Konnichiwa.	●What time is it? It's ... o'clock. ●Be quiet, please. Oh, sorry.
4 At School -English Lesson- 学校で -英語の授業-	●What is this in English? ●It's a stapler.	♪ **The Days of the Week** Sunday, Monday, Tuesday, Wednesday, Thursday, Friday, Saturday	●May I use your eraser? OK. Here you are. ●Take out your textbook. Open it to page eight. OK.
5 On the School Ground 学校のグラウンドで	●Let's play soccer. ●Yes, let's.	♪ **The Action song** walk, hop, skip, dance, swim, fly	●May we go out to play? Sure. ●Go! Run! Kick the ball. Don't stop! Get the ball.
6 At the School Cafeteria 学校のカフェテリアで	●Are you hungry? ●Yes, I am. I'm starving. ●Me, too.	♪ **The Feeling song** happy, angry, brave, sad, merry, hungry, tired	●Two apples, please. OK. Here you are. ●Excuse me. Wait a minute. Get in line. Oh, I'm sorry.
7 At the School Physical 身体検査	●Can you see this letter? ●Yes, I can. It's a "D".	♪ **Head, Shoulders, Knees and Toes** head, shoulders, knees, toes, eyes, ears, mouth, nose	●How tall are you? I'm 140cm tall. ●How much do you weigh? It's a secret.
8 In the School Garden 学校菜園で	●What a wonderful day! ●Look! What a big pumpkin!	♪ **The Weather song** sunny, rainy, windy, snowy, hot, cold	●How many tomatoes do you have...? I have nine tomatoes. ●Please come and help me! I'm coming.
9 On Sunday with My Family ケイトリンの家族の日曜日	●Grandma, do you want some coffee? ●Yes, please. Thank you.	♪ **The Family song** father, mother, brother, sister, grandpa, grandma, dogs, cats	●Dad, where are you? I'm in the garage. ●Have you finished? Almost.
10 At the Supermarket スーパーマーケットで	●We need eggs, milk, bread and sugar. ●Let's buy some strawberries. OK.	♪ **The Twelve Months of the Year** January, February, March, April, May, June, July, August, September, October, November, December	●This watermelon looks good. Let's buy one. ●How much is it? Twenty dollars, please.

	B		C	
	Words	**Phonics**	**Chant**	**Global Education**
	orange, blue, green, pink, brown, yellow, black, red / one, two, three, four, five, six, seven, eight, nine, ten	**大文字 A-Z** Clap your hands with…	▪ This is Canada. ▪ Let's say Hello. (Mexico, Thailand, China, Japan)	**Self-Expression** This is me. My name is… I am … years old. I live in…
	bag, cap, pants, shirt, shoes, skirt, sneakers, sweater, bike, flag, school, school bus, cloud, flower, sun, tree	**小文字 a-z** You (U) are out.	▪ My name is Kaetlyn. ▪ What's your name? ▪ I'm Kaetlyn.You're Eric.	**My School** This is my school. I go to school by bus.
	teacher, student, blackboard, chair, desk, door, light, window, 11~20	**Let's hunt.**	▪ Tick, tock, tick, tock, what time is it? ▪ Shool time, study time. ▪ It's nine o'clock. ♪ **This is my friend**	**My Friends** This is my friend. Her / His name is… (Their names are …)
	chalk, eraser, pencil, pencil case, ruler, scissors, stapler, textbook, English, Japanese, math, music, P.E., science, social studies, Life Environment Studies	**a, b, c, d の音と その文字から始まる語彙** apple, ant, bear, bat, cow, coin, dog, doll	▪ What is this in English? ▪ A stapler. ▪ Once more, please. ▪ Louder, please.	**My Textbook** This is my textbook. I like social studies.
	run, climb, kick, catch, throw, slide, swing, jungle gym, slide, swing, horizontal bar, monkey bars, baseball, basketball, dodgeball, soccer, volleyball	**e, f, g, h の音と その文字から始まる語彙** egg, elephant, fish, fork, goat, ghost, hat, house	▪ Break time. ▪ Are you ready? ▪ Let's go out. ▪ Let's run. ▪ Let's climb. Let's play dodgeball.	**My House** This is my house. I live in Vancouver, Canada.
	apple, fried chicken, hamburger, milk, orange juice, pizza, salad, sandwich, spaghetti, fork, glass, knife, plate, spoon, table, tray	**i, j, k, l の音と その文字から始まる語彙** ink, Indian, jet, jack-o-lantern, king, kite, lion, lemon	▪ Let's eat lunch. ▪ Yum, yum, yum. ▪ Wash your hands and get a tray. ▪ A fork, a knife, a glass and a plate. ▪ I like pizza, salad and milk.	**My Lunch** This is my lunch. I like fried curry shrimp and fried chicken.
	arms, chin, face, feet, fingers, hair, hands, legs, teeth, 20, 30, 40, 50, 60, 70, 80, 90, 100	**m, n, o, p の音と その文字から始まる語彙** monkey, monster, nest, notebook, octopus, orange, pig, pajamas	▪ With my eyes, I can see. ▪ With my ears, I can hear. ▪ With my nose, I can smell. ▪ With my mouth, I can talk. ▪ With my legs, I can walk. ▪ And with your love, what can you do?	**My Treasures** These are my treasures. They are ice skates. (Superman / a beaver / a bear and a mouse)
	cabbage, carrot, cucumber, corn, green pepper, lettuce, onion, potato, pumpkin, tomato, big / little, ant, dragonfly, caterpillar, bird, grasshopper, spider	**q, r, s, t, u の音と その文字から始まる語彙** queen, question, rabbit, ring, sun, Santa, tiger, tree, umbrella, upside down	▪ It's sunny today. Open the window. Feel the sun. ▪ It's rainy today. Open the window. Feel the rain. ▪ It's windy today. Open the window. Feel the wind.	**My Favorite Animals** I want to meet a reindeer walking on the snow. I want to meet a toucan flying in the rain forest. I want to meet a tiger sleeping in the woods. I want to meet a killer whale swimming in the ocean.
	bed, wheelchair, curtain, sofa, telephone, television, video games, bathtub, bathroom, bedroom, living room, kitchen, garage, garden, chimney, roof	**v, w, x, y, z の音と その文字から始まる語彙** violin, volcano, witch, watch, box, fox, yard, yacht, zebra, zoo	▪ Where's Dad? He's in the garage. ▪ What's he doing? Washing his car. ▪ Where's Mom? She's in the kitchen. ▪ What's she doing? Making our lunch. ▪ Where's grandpa? He's in the yard. ▪ What's he doing? Taking a nap.	**My Family** This is my familly. My mother, my father, my brother, and my dog. (my sisters / my parrot)
	banana, orange, pineapple, strawberry, watermelon, bread, egg, cake, meat, sugar, toothbrush, towel, soap, umbrella	**Three-letter words** cat, map, bed, net, pig, lip, box, mop, sun, cup	▪ Let's take a look. In the market, what can you see? I can see carrots. What can you see? I can see eggs. What can you see? ▪ In the zoo, what can you see? (monkeys, lions) ▪ In the school, what can you see? (blackboard, teacher)	**More about Myself** My birthday is … I like playing the piano. I am good at skating. I want to be a piano teacher.

Country Profile

CANADA

Area	9,985,000 km^2
Capital	Ottawa
Population	38 million people
Languages	English and French
Money	Canadian dollar ● 1 dollar = 100 cents

Canadian **dollar**

MEXICO

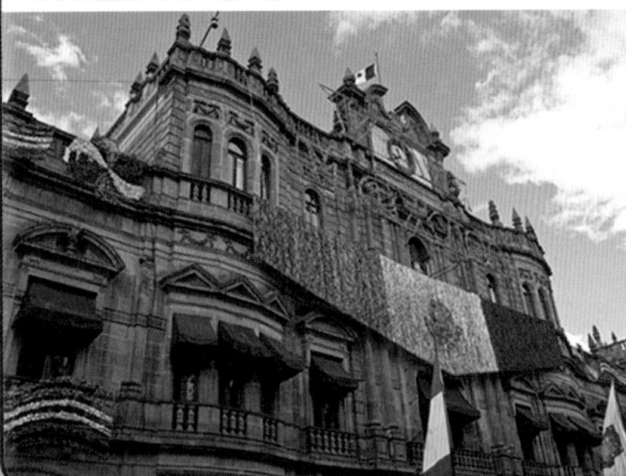

Area	1,973,000 km^2
Capital	Mexico City
Population	129.7 million people
Language	Spanish
Money	Peso ● 1 peso = 100 centavos

Mexican **peso**

THAILAND

Area	513,100 km^2
Capital	Bangkok
Population	69.9 million people
Language	Thai
Money	Baht ● 1 baht = 100 satang

Thai **baht**

CHINA

Area	9,597,000 km^2
Capital	Beijing
Population	1.44 billion people
Language	Chinese
Money	Yuan（元） ● 1 yuan = 10 jiao

My name is

PROGRESS REPORT

4	6	8	10	12	14	16	18	20	22
24	26	28	30	32	34	36	38	40	42
44	46	48	50	52	54	56	58	60	62

★ Challenge Chart ★

Date	1	2	3	4	5	6	7	8	9	10	11	12	Total

Date	1	2	3	4	5	6	7	8	9	10	11	12	Total

先生の質問にこたえて色をぬりましょう。

Students color in one happy face at a time on answering each of the teacher's questions during warm up/review time.

Certificate of Achievement

Awarded to ____________________________

this __________ *day of* ____________, ________

for your great effort in

READY for Learning World

Signed